Atypical Girl Geek

Atypical Girl Geek

A Memoir

Katherine A. Hitchcock

Published by Volant Press
www.VolantPress.com

Print ISBN: 978-0-9961905-0-3
eBook ISBN: 978-0-9961905-1-0

Cover & interior photographs © Katherine A. Hitchcock
Cover photo: Celebration of the IBM's Paper Recycling Program, 1971
Frontispiece: Graduation photo, University of Washington, 1965
Back cover photo: Hiking in Zermat, Switzerland, 1969

Interior Book Design
Jeff Duckworth/Duck of All Trades: www.duckofalltrades.com

Cover Design & Book Production
Eva Long/Long on Books: www.longonbooks.com

Hitchcock, Katherine A.
    Atypical girl geek : a memoir / Katherine A. Hitchcock.
    pages : illustrations ; cm

    Issued also as an ebook.
    Includes bibliographical references.
    ISBN: 978-0-9961905-0-3 (print)

    1. Hitchcock, Katherine A.--Career in computer programming. 2.
International Business Machines Corporation--Employees. 3. Women
computer programmers. 4. Women in technology. 5. Autobiography. I.
Title.

QA76.2.H58 A3 2015

005.1092

Printed in U.S.A.

To the memory of Edmund 'Bear' Downing
and to my stepchildren,
Todd, Sara and Gavin

Atypical: Not conforming to the type.

Girl: A young woman.

Geek: A person that utilizes new technologies to do interesting or useful things.

Contents

Prologue

On a hot August day in 2011, I sat visiting with a friend in the shade of a grand old apricot tree. She was puzzling over the next step in her career and I was providing a listening ear. She had worked for Microsoft as a project manager then had taken time to raise her young family. Now she was looking to go back to work. At some point I started to share some stories from my long career with IBM. With her encouragement I kept talking, and story after story poured out of me.

Her face lit up with interest as she listened. "Have you written these down?" she asked.

"No, I haven't," I replied.

"Well, you should. You witnessed some pretty interesting things in the history of computers. I think you should record what you saw."

A seed was planted that hot afternoon. Then in September I attended a Guided Autobiography class where our first assignment was to write about a turning point in our lives. I wrote about a turning point at IBM. Another assignment was about how we discovered our profession, which took me back to my senior year in college and to the chance encounter that led me to programming and to IBM. All in all we wrote on a dozen different topics in that class.

Still I was not thinking about it very seriously until I emailed these stories to my brother Les. As he read them, his comment was "Keep them coming." My nephews and stepsons, all of them very tech savvy in their own way, always listened with interest when I shared anything about my career. "Perhaps there *is* some interest in my story," I thought.

Then I remembered the stories written by my father's family. Both his father and grandfather wrote about their life journey. As I have gotten older I have read these stories with more interest, stories that described their lives in the late nineteenth and the early twentieth centuries. In particular I learned that my great-grandfather ran a newspaper in Vancouver, Washington, where my grandfather, as a teenager, learned the skills of typesetting that led to his printing business in Seattle in the early part of the twentieth century. I recognized continuity: that I, his granddaughter, wrote computer programs to drive high-speed printers and experimental printers in the late twentieth century. In their tradition they wrote not a detailed autobiography but a description of the course of their careers. This set me thinking again about my path through IBM.

So I began.

This is my journey of thirty-five years working as a computer programmer with IBM—from arriving fresh out of college in 1966 to retiring as a senior programmer in 2001. When I began at IBM there were no computer science departments at colleges or universities. Few people interacted with computers. Today, as we know, it is a completely different story. I watched and participated in the step-by-step development of computer technology beginning with very primitive tools. I witnessed the spark of ideas that grew into commonplace products that we encounter everyday: the supermarket barcode and the ATM machine to name just two.

I saw all this from the inside the corporate structure of IBM. Often a large corporation is seen from the outside as a monolithic structure. But these stereotypes do not reflect the actual individual experiences. Inside IBM I encountered amazingly talented people working on forward-thinking projects with innovative ideas that contributed to the computer technological revolution that has reshaped our society. This is the story of my contribution, how I wove my unique path—all the twists and turns, all the ups and downs, all the failures and successes—and found my way to a rewarding career at IBM while learning valuable life lessons.

During these same years I witnessed a growing environmental awareness in myself, corporations, and society. But corporate and society awareness is the result of the actions of individuals. In addition to my technical contributions, this is the story of how my actions initiated a recycling program, in 1969, and a carpooling program, in 1971, within IBM.

These are my memories and like all memories they are subject to error. All events and experiences herein are all true to the best of my recollection, while the quoted conversations represent my best re-construction. Any errors or omissions are unintentional and are completely my responsibility. This is how I saw and participated, in my small way, in the development of computer technology in the twentieth century.

1965
Finding My Profession

It was a warm, sunny, August afternoon as I walked across the University of Washington (UW) campus in Seattle. Mt. Rainier stood out boldly in the distance. The year was 1965 and I was about to enter my senior year. I was beginning to wonder what I would do when I graduated. What kinds of jobs were available for someone graduating with a Bachelor of Science in Mathematics?

Math had always come easily to me. In my fourth and fifth grades, I had had the good fortune of attending the Payne Training Grade School associated with Arizona State in Tempe, Arizona. In this progressive school, the students were encouraged and allowed to learn at their own rate. When we were ready to be tested on our assignments, our spelling words or our multiplication tables, we raised our hand and one of the many student teachers came over and tested us individually. When we successfully passed the test for one level we could get the sheet to study for the next level. The mimeographed sheets of paper with the times tables were located in the cabinet at the edge of the room. I remember one whispered conversation at the cabinet.

"I'm on my sixes, what are you on?"

"I'm on my sevens!"

We had a friendly competition to learn them all. I remember one day when a classmate was having trouble with her assignment. She was upset and crying. I sat with her and calmed her while explaining how that level of multiplication worked.

So it was not surprising that in high school, looking ahead to college, I had decided to become a math teacher. But my father and my high school math teacher coached me, both recommending that I major in math and minor in education instead of majoring in education. They said that I would have more opportunities with a degree in math.

Growing up, my father was in the US Army and we moved every few years, but we lived in one place for my last three years of high school: El Paso, Texas. As I graduated my father was going on an overseas assignment, while my mother and younger siblings—I was one of six children—stayed in El Paso until his return. If there was anyplace we called home it was Seattle, Washington, where both my parents grew up. When I looked around to choose a university I was strongly influenced by the fact that I qualified for Washington in-state tuition—because of my father's retained residency—and by the invitation from my aunt and uncle to live in their home. My older brother, John, accepted a similar invitation the previous year and he was living with them while studying electrical engineering. Thus I found my way to the Department of Mathematics at the University of Washington, arriving in time for the 1962 Seattle Worlds Fair.

During my first three years, I was engrossed with my math classes and delayed taking the education courses. Looking at the catalog of available classes each quarter I always favored the math classes over the education classes, anyway. But this brought up the question: If I wasn't going to be a math teacher, what was I going to be?

Seeking the answer, I headed to the School of Business in Mackenzie Hall that August day. There were two placement offices on UW campus: one located on the lower campus for the engineering students and one located in the School of Business. When I inquired at the engineering placement office, I was told that recruiters would visit the campus in the spring but they could not tell me anything now about job opportunities. So I decided to try the placement office in the School of Business. When I arrived, I told them I was looking to see what job opportunities were available to someone graduating with a degree in math. The woman behind the counter became very animated and told me there was a professor looking for someone to work for him, and that I had the exact qualifications he was looking for. I told her that I already had a part-time job and that I was looking for job opportunities when I graduated.

But she insisted, "Go upstairs and talk with him. Right now."

Upstairs, at the end of the long hall, I turned left and found Professor William F. Sharpe, a bespectacled man in his early thirties with sandy brown hair, sitting in his office. The room was small with a messy desk on the left and a large blackboard on the wall to the right. Straight ahead, next to the window, was a guest chair. Dr. Sharpe, I learned, was a professor of economics in the Business School. With animation he outlined his plans to teach his business students about the capabilities and limitations of computers. At that time all the computers were located in a building on the southern part of the campus near the engineering departments, which was about half a mile away. Dr. Sharpe wanted his business students to have the convenience of turning in their computer programs and picking up their output in the business school building, at the north edge of campus. He was opening a small office and he needed someone to manage it. In addition, he was looking for someone to write some programs for other business school professors. Did I want the job? Starting now?

I was not too interested—after all, I already had a part-time job—but I told him I would think about it.

That evening over dinner at home with John, Aunt Lois, and Uncle Lee, I shared the story of my day. I related it as an interesting experience but I was still focused on what I would do after graduation and not thinking about changing jobs.

For the past year I had been working twenty hours a week doing statistical calculations for a research project at Providence Hospital. Scientists there were conducting early research into finding a heart replacement valve. Pages and pages of handwritten data documented the chemical components of blood samples taken during surgery and they wanted to know if there was a correlation between different components in the blood and body temperature. I used a mechanical calculator and entered the data, by hand, to perform the statistical calculations. Earlier that week I had spoken with my boss at the hospital, someone I rarely saw.

"I've been here a year and I don't have any correlations to report," I told him.

"These things take time, it's the nature of research. Don't be discouraged," he replied, assuring me that he was pleased with my work.

As I left the meeting I thought to myself, "If that's what research is like, then I'm not too interested. I like the satisfaction of getting results."

Slowly, during the dinner discussion with my aunt, uncle, and brother, I changed my focus from the future to considering this current opportunity with Dr. Sharpe. I reflected on the tedious work at the hospital doing statistical calculations with little results. I liked the idea of working on campus since my current job required me to take two buses and transfer, often in the rain. By the next morning I had decided to take the job.

That is how I started to work for Dr. Sharpe and the business students. I kept the School of Business remote computer office open as the students came by to use the keypunch machine and drop off their stacks of computer cards. Some students were learning to write BASIC[1] computer programs, and they keypunched each instruction into an IBM card. Other students were taking a class that used the computer to simulate a competitive business environment. These students were divided into teams and each team represented a different imaginary company. The teams made decisions about how much to spend in various areas of their business (research, manufacturing, infrastructure, advertising). These numbers were keypunched into computer cards to be used as input to the simulation program. The program then printed out the results of how their company did in the competitive business environment with the other teams. But first, all the cards needed to be taken to the computer center where they were the "input" to the simulation program running on the computer.

Another student worked as the courier but occasionally I took the programs down to the main computing facility. Here, I walked into a room with keypunch machines lining each wall. At the counter I dropped off my batches of already keypunched cards. Behind the counter I looked through a window into the large room with raised floors. Big grey computers, looking like tall cabinets, stood in rows down the middle of the room. Along the left wall were more tall cabinets with spinning reels of magnetic tape. Hidden under the raised floors were large black cables that connected the different computer cabinets. I learned that the computer room was always air-conditioned because of the heat given off by the electronic machines.

I walked over to the "output" section, which was a wall of pigeonhole boxes. Here I picked up the results of the computer runs to take back to the School of Business remote computer office. A rubber band strapped a computer listing around each original stack of cards. The computer listing consisted of lined, legal-sized, fan-fold[2] computer paper with a printout of the program showing either the successful results or a list of errors.

The previous school year I had taken a computer class offered by the math department and I found it very dull and uninteresting. Focused so much on the internal addressing mechanism of computers, this class was a little like studying the wiring diagram for a car but never getting the overall picture of a car and its capabilities. There was no computer science department at the university in 1965, only a scattering of computer-related classes in the engineering and math departments.

It was around this time that my father recommended that I consider becoming a computer programmer. He said it was probably a good career for women because it was a brand new field. I told him I wasn't interested. I could not see much to recommend those big grey cabinets inside the air-conditioned room with the raised floors.

Then one day a business student came by to pick up his computer listing and he expressed disappointment because it did not work as he expected. There was some kind of error and he did not know what was wrong. I looked at the listing and I could see the error immediately. I had never seen anything written in this particular computer language but I could see that the logic was incorrect. It seemed that I could just understand it. It was beginning to dawn on me that I had some natural ability in this area.

This revelation continued to be affirmed when Dr. Sharpe would discuss computer ideas with me, which he often did when he needed to talk out a problem. He was in the process of writing a new and improved compiler for BASIC and he would stand at his blackboard describing all the intricate steps of how the compiler worked. I would sit there and look at the diagrams he created and listen to his explanations.

I would follow his logic until it stopped making sense to me. Then I would get a frown on my face and interrupt him to say something like: "But previously you said it went this way and now you are saying something completely different."

He would exclaim, "That's why it's not working!" and quickly usher me out of his office as he resumed working on his compiler.

Dr. Sharpe was on the committee to buy computers for the university, and one day he invited me to a demonstration of a new computing system. We drove to an office building in downtown Seattle, where we entered a small room that was entirely empty except for a desk in the middle. On the desk was a telephone and something that looked like a typewriter. This typewriter was really a remote computer terminal and it was connected by phone lines to a computer at General Electric in Phoenix, Arizona. As we typed simple formulas, 10 + 77 for example, the numbers were transmitted across the phone lines to the computer that calculated the answer and transmitted the result back to the typewriter terminal in the office: 87. This was remote computing.

As I watched this and realized what was happening, it was as if a light bulb went off in my head and I got very excited. I could imagine the business students entering their data into this typewriter terminal and getting the results from their simulation program typed back to them immediately. No more keypunched computer cards, courier trips to the computer center, and long delays before getting the results.

"This is the way computers should work," I thought. "They should provide the answers at our fingertips." Suddenly I saw computers in a new light and I knew then that I would apply for a job as a computer programmer.

1966
Job Opportunities

I n the spring of my senior year I went to the engineering placement center and submitted my application for a job as a computer programmer. Within a week I had lined up several preliminary interviews. These initial interviews took place on campus with a recruiter from the various corporations. If there was sufficient mutual interest, I would be invited to travel to their location for further interviews.

This was an exciting time and my attention was on interviewing, not on studying. I frequented the placement center and met with the various recruiters, among them men who represented Boeing, IBM in Seattle and San Jose, the Rand Corporation in Santa Monica, and the computer division of General Electric (GE) in Phoenix. All five of these organizations invited me for a second interview at their location.

First I interviewed with Boeing, but I remember very little about it.

Next I met with the IBM sales division in downtown Seattle and learned something about a position called "Systems Engineer." Systems Engineers provided technical support for the sales team, as well as technical assistance to the IBM customers once they had purchased a computer system. The sales team and the Systems Engineers were the most visible aspect of IBM since they interacted with the customers. These IBM employees were always professionally dressed in suits and ties, for indeed most were men, giving the world the impression that IBM had a white shirt dress code.

Then I traveled to Arizona to interview with GE. My maternal grandparents lived in Phoenix where they settled, seeking warmer weather, after they retired from the Seattle School District—my grandfather as a well respected high-school math teacher, my grandmother as a nutritionist for the public school lunch program. I was happy to visit my grandparents and share my job hunting experiences with them. I was looking forward to learning more about GE since this was the company that had demonstrated remote computing to Dr. Sharpe and me earlier in the year.

But I was disappointed when I arrived. I walked into a large warehouse or manufacturing building with offices for the computer programmers on the second floor overlooking these activities. No one was talking about remote computing and the ideas I found exciting.

When I arrived for my interview with IBM in San Jose, California, I stayed in a small downtown hotel that the company had booked for me. I then drove south down Monterey Highway, a divided highway with large trees planted in the median, to the IBM Cottle Road location. I met with the personnel manager who showed me my schedule for the day. He had planned five or six interviews for me with different department managers in divisions whose names were abbreviated to initials: SMD and SDD. I felt like

I was in a new and unfamiliar world where everything was encoded in acronyms and technical jargon.

At my first interview the previous applicant was just leaving and there was an animated discussion going on between the managers. It seems that this applicant, a woman, was staying at the same hotel where I was staying and had reported that the night clerk had propositioned her. Naturally, she was upset and the managers were discussing the appropriateness of the hotel that IBM had selected. I was asked if this had happened to me. I thought back to the previous evening and the strange behavior of the night clerk. He seemed flakey and unprofessional but I did not have a problem with him. If he attempted to solicit me, I was too naive to notice.

I began my interviews. In each department I met with several people who described their projects. But with all the new terms I was hearing, I could not make heads or tails of them. I did not know the difference between manufacturing support or development. And why were they always saying "systems"? It seemed like everything was about this system or that system. Since I had limited knowledge of corporations and their internal structure, I could not distinguish the function of one group from another.

At the end of the day, around 5 p.m., I again met with the personnel manager for a closing interview. He asked me my opinion of the different departments and projects. I could hardly form one; my head was spinning with new impressions.

He pressured me to select one. "Would you take a job with this group if it was offered to you?"

How could I answer that at the end of this busy day of interviewing? I could not give him a definitive answer so I finally said, "I am waiting to see what other offers I receive before I make a decision."

Later, on reflection, I understood that he wanted to know if I would accept the offer before he went through all the paperwork to extend it.

As I left his office I walked to the large parking lot that extended for a couple of blocks in either direction. I stood, looking out over the landscape, and wondered. "Would I like to take a job here? Would I like to work here?" I crossed to my rental car and drove back north along Monterey Highway with its elegant trees.

My interview with the Rand Corporation in Santa Monica was partly thanks to Dr. Sharpe, who had worked there at an earlier time in his career. I was favorably impressed with the facility and the people I met there. However, Dr. Sharpe had told me that with only a Bachelor of Science degree in math I would probably be assigned tasks like cutting out articles from technical journals or magazines, which constituted information gathering and saving before online computer search engines. He indicated that I would need a more advanced degree to continue with Rand, since PhDs did most of the interesting work.

Back on campus, Dr. Sharpe knew most of the recruiters from the different companies. I learned that when he saw one of them he would comment about the offers I was receiving from the other companies. "Oh, I understand you're interviewing Kathy Hitchcock. She has a great offer from the Rand Corporation, and IBM, and..."

So I had someone campaigning for me. If that influenced the amount of money I was being offered I never knew, but soon I had five respectable job offers. This was the spring of 1966 and employment opportunities were abundant, especially in the newly developing field of computer programming.

Now it was time for me to choose which job to accept. As I faced this decision it became clear to me that no one was going to give me any advice on what or how to choose. My father did not voice an opinion, my aunt and uncle refrained from offering advice, and even Dr. Sharpe maintained a neutral stance. Everyone was very interested in the outcome, but they were adamant that it needed to be my decision.

At home Aunt Lois, Uncle Lee or John decided to make a lottery out of which job I would choose. They wrote the names of the five offers on separate pieces of paper and sealed them inside envelopes. Then they sold the envelopes for $1 a piece. Whoever's envelope contained the name of the company that I selected would receive the $5 prize. No one knew what was written inside the envelope they purchased so they could not influence my decision. Even Dr. Sharpe bought one.

I quickly eliminated the two job offers in Seattle: the Boeing offer and IBM Systems Engineer position. After my four university years in Seattle the winters were too dreary and rainy for me and I wanted warmer weather. I also eliminated the job offer with GE in Phoenix based on the sterile industrial feel of their building and offices. This left me with two offers to consider, and they were both in California. These two offers were in cities where I did not know anyone, but at the time this did not even register with me. Growing up in a military family, I had moved dozens of times in my life, so this was just another move, I thought.

I compared these two job offers with their different settings and opportunities. One was with a major computer company, the other a small think tank. I thought back over my recent trip to the Rand Corporation in Santa Monica. I remembered arriving at the large LA International Airport and driving the confusing streets to my interview. The facility was small and attractive. The people were friendly and enthusiastic about their projects even though I did not understand their work. I knew it was a prestigious firm and I was honored to have an offer. I was leaning toward taking this position.

The other offer was with IBM in San Jose. I liked the feel of San Jose. The airport was easy to negotiate. I liked the tree-lined boulevard that led to the IBM location on the Monterey Highway. I later learned that these trees were planted during the days of the Spanish missions in California along the roads that connected the missions. My offer was with the Systems Manufacturing Division of IBM. This meant that I would be writing programs to support the manufacturing activities, but that did not tell me very much about what I would be doing.

Late one evening I finally decided. I would accept the offer from the Rand Corporation. Before telling anyone I wanted to sleep on the decision and see if it still felt right in the morning.

When I woke the next morning, I reconsidered. I thought IBM San Jose would be a better decision. I based this on two factors: 1) I remembered what Dr. Sharpe said about needing an advanced degree for the Rand Corporation, and 2) I felt there was so much that I needed to learn and IBM was prepared to train me. So I choose the manufacturing support programming job with IBM in San Jose.

I walked into the kitchen that morning to announce my long and agonized decision. My aunt was making a wonderful breakfast, as she did each morning.

"I have decided what job to take," I announced as I entered.

Before I could say more my aunt interrupted me saying, "Wait, let me find my envelope."

That was the reaction of everyone I told throughout the day. Even Dr. Sharpe, when I stopped by his office to tell him, opened his drawer and searched for the envelope before I could share my decision. So while it was a life changing decision for me, others were mostly interested in whether they had won the $5 prize.

Reflecting back on this period in my life, I realize I owe a debt of gratitude to Dr. Sharpe. Later, after he moved to California and joined the Stanford Business School, we had lunch a couple of times. Imagine my surprise and delight one day in 1990 when I opened the newspaper to read that he had won the Nobel Prize for Economics[3]. I immediately called to extend my congratulations. He won this prize for work that he had done before I knew him, work that he did at the Rand Corporation.

1966-1968
First Assignments

After I accepted the job offer from IBM, I received a letter informing me that if I started work before July 1st, I would be eligible to participate in the IBM Stock Purchase Plan. Looking at this information and not wanting to miss out on this opportunity for an entire year, I selected Monday, June 27, 1966 as my starting date. My starting salary was $675 per month. I was twenty-one years old. But first I needed to finish my senior year and graduate.

For the last two years my family had lived nearby, just south of Tacoma, Washington, while my father worked at McChord Air Force Base. But now we were going in three different directions: I to IBM in San Jose, California; John, with his EE degree and ROTC commission, to begin his career in the Army; my parents and younger siblings to McLean, Virginia, where my father was starting a new assignment in Washington, D.C.

After the mid-June graduation ceremonies, I left Seattle accompanied by my sister, Melinda, in my new car: a metallic-pink Oldsmobile Cutlass, nicknamed the Pink Panther. We drove to San Francisco and rendezvoused with my mother and my three younger brothers—Les, Keith, and Luther—who had left a few days behind us. After a short visit with family friends, we all drove to San Jose. It was an exciting time for me as I quickly hugged everyone, waved farewell, and checked into the Hyatt Hotel. My mother left to drive my four younger siblings to Virginia. Little did I know that I would only see my mother one more time.

IBM had arranged accommodations for me at the Hyatt Hotel—a much better hotel than the one they selected when I interviewed—until I could find an apartment. The following day I began work at the IBM Cottle Road location as a junior programmer for the Systems Manufacturing Division (SMD). That evening I looked for an apartment. I found one just a few miles down the road from the IBM location, but it was not available for a few days—not until the first week of July.

After two days at the hotel, alone, I became homesick. As an Army brat, I had moved dozens of times in my life, but always my family was with me. Now I was alone in a new city with a new job and I did not know anyone. I had not anticipated this first experience of loneliness in the evening when I returned from work. But that soon changed when I met a family staying at the hotel who invited me to join them for dinners.

Later in the week another woman, Cathy Jones, a graduate in math from Colorado College, started work in my area at IBM. She, too, was looking for an apartment but in Palo Alto or Mountain View, because she had heard that these cities were a better place to live than south San Jose if you were single. Together, over the Fourth of July weekend, we checked out the apartment situation in these two cities, and quickly saw the advantage of rooming together. We found a two-bedroom apartment, with pool, in Mountain View about 30 miles north of the IBM Cottle Road location and I let go of the one-bedroom apartment in San Jose.

Cathy and I roomed together for three years. It was very good for my social life to room with her and we soon met two guys, both Stanford graduate students, who shared our interest in hiking and skiing. We practiced our cooking skills by hosting a dinner once a week for them.

We also met three more women, new IBM employees, who lived in Mountain View and worked at the same location. Two were programmers and one was in the Personnel Department. We started a five-person carpool, commuting from Mountain View to San Jose on US Highway 101. We each drove one day a week and our carpool continued in some shape or form for a few years.

When we arrived at work we punched a time card. The start times were staggered and the hour was broken into tenths of an hour. Our starting time was 7:42 a.m. To be prompt we left Mountain View before 7 a.m.

During those first weeks I attended several orientation classes. In one I learned the history of IBM's beginnings in San Jose. Just ten years earlier a small group of IBM scientists and engineers had invented the disk drive technology, an important advancement. Before disk drives, the external or secondary storage for computers was either on a magnetic drum or a magnetic tape. The data on a magnetic drum could be accessed directly, allowing quick data retrieval, but the drum was physically limited in its data capacity. The magnetic tape, on the other hand, had unlimited capacity, but required that the data be accessed sequentially, resulting in slower data retrieval. The IBM engineers solved the technical problems of reading and writing on magnetically coated disks—a stack of disks spinning at high speed—to create the RAMAC[4], the first random access disk storage device in 1956.

This technology had led to the construction of the IBM Cottle Road location. Prior to that, this large piece of property was a farm with orchards. The farmhouse still stood at the edge of the property across from acres of parking lots and large manufacturing buildings. Inside these manufacturing buildings a team of employees assembled the disk drives while another team worked in special clean rooms—a dust-free environment—to coat the magnetic disks. Another building provided office space for the engineers who designed improvements, enhancements, and innovations to the disk technology. One building contained a research lab and another one an education center. This IBM San Jose Cottle Road facility was the headquarters for the disk drive division, the only IBM division headquarters that was not in New York. All these things were in existence when I arrived in 1966.

My workspace was located in a large, open, high-ceiling manufacturing building called Building 5. I walked through a maze of passageways to my work area: a desk with a bookshelf attached to its back to provide privacy from the desks in front and behind. My neighbor's desk was adjacent to mine separated by a file cabinet. These desks and bookshelves provided a rabbit-like labyrinth where we worked. The computer, an IBM 1401[5], was at the other end of the building running batch jobs[6]. Each job contained a set of instructions keypunched into IBM cards, the cards were read and processed by the computer that then printed a computer listing containing the results. The computer operator prioritized and scheduled the jobs by loading the punched cards into the card reader. It was always a good idea to be on friendly terms with the computer operator who had the ability to expedite your program in the queue. The computer processed one job at a time. Remote computing had not begun yet. In order to submit a batch job or pick up my output, I had to walk the length of the building through this labyrinth. I often thought this was a test: if you could not find your way through this maze, then you were probably not smart enough to work here.

My first assignment was to modify a batch program written in Autocoder[7]. The program was one of many that involved purchasing and tracking the parts for manufacturing the disk drives. It had something to do with the bill of materials[8] process that specified the component parts for the disk drives including how many nuts, screws, and bolts were needed to put it together. The technical leader in our department gave me this assignment and when I asked him about the documentation for the program he said, "There is none. Find out what it does by reading the code." I sat at my desk, almost falling asleep, studying this obscure code. Weeks later, when I had figured everything out, this same guy gave me the documentation. I looked at him dumbfounded, since he had told me there was none. He said, "I wanted you to learn that the code is the reality, not what the documentation says." That was my first lesson.

IBM was expanding quickly and hiring new people. Soon they ran out of space in Building 5 and our department moved to the old farmhouse that was located on the edge of the IBM property. This increased the distance between my office and the other buildings: it was now a two or three block walk to the cafeteria or to the computer in Building 5. My desk, with the attached bookshelf, was moved to the dining room in the farmhouse. Being the only woman in the department, the five or six men expected me to fix the morning coffee. I didn't drink coffee but made an attempt to comply until they figured out that they were better off doing it themselves.

With my roommate, Cathy, and new friends, we spent our weekends in the Sierra Nevada—backpacking in the summer and skiing in the winter. At the end of one of my first backpacking trips I was reluctant to return to civilization on Sunday afternoon. We had followed a trail across Hetch Hetchy Reservoir, under a waterfall, and up along a creek in Yosemite National Park. The beauty of the wilderness held my attention. "I'd like to sit next to that tree," I wished, "and write my computer programs from here."

But that wasn't possible at the time, so I returned to the office and continued working on my Autocoder programs. With all the comings and goings in the farmhouse, sometimes I would be the only one there. One day, one of my male colleagues walked in and made a suggestive comment about us being the only two alone in a farmhouse. Recognizing the bait but not biting, I focused on my project and ignored him. When summer came, those of us working in the farmhouse had ideas about having BBQ lunches. One man, who worked in the bedroom/office upstairs and was designing the requirements for the new purchasing system, developed a flowchart[9] on how to have a BBQ in 42 minutes, since that was the length of our lunch hour. Flowcharts were one way of describing the flow of logic in a computer program and in this case he created a practical and humorous chart for cooking and eating lunch. The flowchart specified that someone start BBQ coals during the morning break, and then listed the sequence of tasks during lunch: cook, eat, cleanup, and visit. The flowchart had a diamond-shaped decision block that told us to check the time and specified "return to work" when lunchtime was over. We had fun trying to fit everything into the allotted time. It was hard for management to keep track of us since we were off on the edge of the property, but we were intent on maintaining our time commitments. Within a year my department was moved to one of the new trailers and we left the farmhouse, the most unusual place that I ever worked.

IBM announced a new programming language, PL/I, which was written for the IBM System 360. PL/I stands for Programming Language One, not a very exciting name. One of my colleagues, Burt Swanson, organized and taught a series of classes on PL/I and I was a student in the first series. At the end Burt asked me to teach the next one. He indicated that he only wanted to teach it once as a way of learning PL/I for himself. I taught the series several times in a row to the newly arriving programmers in our area. Then I taught it as part of the IBM Continuing Education program that was offered at the beautiful new IBM Education Center, the entrance of which displayed a quote from IBM founder Thomas J. Watson: "There is no saturation point to education." This class was available to anyone working at IBM and I taught it in the evening, in addition to my normal work assignments, for a couple of years. I strongly recommended that each student come to class with a problem he or she wanted to solve using PL/I. I felt that, if they had a specific use for PL/I, it would make the class more relevant for them.

Then I was assigned to a remote computing project to design and build an interactive, online purchasing system to be used by all the IBM manufacturing locations. This was an endeavor to eliminate duplicated effort, update the computer programs to the latest hardware and operating system (OS/360[10]), and standardize the purchasing programs and procedures within IBM. We were re-designing the purchasing process from a punched card, batch system to an interactive system using remote display terminals for the purchasing staff. The purchasing department relied on weekly computer runs that printed a stack of fan-fold computer paper containing the information about current inventory. They did not have display terminals on their desks; they did not have the latest inventory information at their fingertips. We were to design the look and feel of the new interactive application that would provide this information for them. The newly hired programmers were assigned to this project, but because it was still in an early design and specification phase, no actual programs were being written.

We were mostly involved in meetings and collecting user requirements for the project. In these meetings I was usually the only woman in a room where most of the men were smoking. Not a smoker myself, these smoke-filled rooms annoyed me but it never occurred to me to complain. The smoking practices changed slowly during my years at IBM: the health risks were publicized; fewer people smoked; dangers of secondhand smoke were recognized; people started to complain; smoking was limited to one side of the meeting room or auditorium; then smoking was eliminated from meeting rooms but you could smoke in your office. Finally, close to twenty-five years later, smoking was prohibited anywhere in the buildings.

Meanwhile, our meetings seemed like a useless exercise to me. No one was writing programs yet and I could not see a reason for teaching PL/I to the new hires who were not even assigned to programming projects. I was frustrated also with the size of the project and my limited view. I could not see that we were making any forward progress. It seemed that nothing got built.

Finally I decided to take a different course of action. With so little direction from management, I set my own. I found or heard about a simulator program for the IBM 2260 display terminal[11]. The IBM 2260 was the display that we were going to use for the purchasing project but no one had used this device before. Since the 2260 display terminal ran on the OS/360 operating system I contacted John Thomas, our resident operating systems specialist, and asked him to build an operating system that included the 2260 device. Today you would download a new device driver from the Internet but back then we had to build the device driver into the operating system from the beginning. He agreed and arranged a block of dedicated computer time early one morning to

27

construct the system. I watched the multiple steps of loading one program, then another, into the computer to build layer after layer of function that created the OS/360 system that could read/write to the 2260 display terminal.

Once I had this OS/360 system, I installed and tested the 2260 simulator. The simulator allowed me to design the layout of the display screens to illustrate the interactive sequence of displays for placing a purchase order. The simulator would switch from one screen to the next based on the keyboard input. This allowed me to provide a sample demonstration of what the interactive purchasing application might look like. I was able to demonstrate this sequence and present it to the purchasing staff as a design tool for narrowing down the data entry requirements. But there was no actual data processing going on behind these screens.

Still the project was so large, in terms of number of people and in terms of scope, that it was difficult to know how to make any forward progress.

One of the new managers made things worse when he left a message on the desk of anyone who was not there on time. "It is 7:42 a.m. and you are not at work." As you can imagine, this angered many of the employees, especially employees who had worked late into the night or arrived early to acquire computer time. Fortunately, that manager didn't last long.

When I discussed my job dissatisfaction with my father or uncle, they both cautioned me to stick it out. Having grown up during the depression years they felt that I was very fortunate to have a job. But, realizing that the times were different, I decided to apply for a transfer within IBM to another assignment. I filled out a Request for Transfer form and turned it into the personnel department. Then I met with the personnel manager who, as I recall, was the same man I had met when I first interviewed with IBM in 1966. He checked for job openings, found one and arranged for me to speak with the manager on a project that was building a new compiler. During the interview I understood that if I came to work on their project I would be assigned the job of testing the compiler. That seemed very limiting, and I had a new appreciation for the variety of tasks and learning experiences I had in my current assignment. So I decided to stay put and continue with the work I was doing.

At this time my mother was ill. Early in 1967 she was diagnosed with colon cancer and it had already metastasized to her liver by the time it was discovered. Neither of my parents wanted me to leave my job and return home to help out. I did what I could from a distance: writing her daily letters. Her letters expressed how proud she was of all her children. When I was home over the Memorial Day weekend, she was weak but trying to be as upbeat as possible. I never understood how serious this illness was and I fully expected to see her when I went home for Christmas. She only lasted until September.

As I recovered from this loss, work matters did not improve. Months later I remember thinking long and hard about applying for a transfer again. In early January 1968, while hiking one weekend with friends, I reviewed the working conditions and debated the options. By the end of the hike, I had decided the situation at work was unacceptable and I would request a transfer. Sunday evening I prepared the paperwork.

Monday morning I arrived at work to discover that I had a new manager: a dynamic young woman who had been with IBM for a few years. Quickly I reviewed my reasons for a transfer and wondered if a new manager would make a difference. But, determined to find a new job, I walked into her office and presented her with my Request for Transfer.

Startled, she asked, "Are you uncomfortable having a woman manager?" She was eager to convince me that we could work together.

"No," I replied. "My concerns are related to the project."

"What are your concerns?" she queried.

Should I really tell her all the things that were wrong with the project? What a way for her to start her new job. Should I really point out all the deficiencies? Starting with hiring and training programmers but not giving them anything to program? But she convinced me that she was interested in hearing everything I had to say and so we had an open and frank conversation.

This was the only time in my IBM career that I worked for a woman manager and I only remember that one meeting with her, but I was impressed with her ability to listen. I wished her well.

When I met with the personnel manager, the same one as before, he looked at me and said, "Are we going to play this game again?"

Looking him directly in the eye I said, "I am serious. If I do not have a new assignment with IBM within a month, then I will go to a different company."

1968-1969
Library Automation Project

This time, when I requested a transfer, there was an opening at the Advanced Systems Development Division (ASDD). They were looking for a programmer and it seemed that my qualifications fit their need. I did not know too much about ASDD but Bob Martin, one of the students in my evening PL/I class, worked there. I asked him if he would stay after class and talk with me and he agreed. Sitting on a table in the back of the classroom, his long legs reached out for a nearby chair as he spoke. "This unique division, founded by Rey Johnson[12] about ten years ago, looks at potential ways for computers to be used in the future," he said. "We focus on the next seven to ten years, or to the mid to late 1970s."

"Who is Rey Johnson?" I queried.

"Rey Johnson was the manager of the project that developed the disk data storage technology. All the IBM manufacturing and development work done here in San Jose is the result of this technology."

This was fascinating. I knew all about the innovative disk technology but I did not know who had worked on it. I was eager to hear more.

"In the early 1950s," Bob continued, "Rey led a small group of IBM engineers working on a research project in

31

downtown San Jose. You have to understand that almost all the IBM corporate offices, manufacturing facilities, research and development labs were located in the New York area. From time to time IBM's upper management would arrive from back east to review the project. They canceled it more than once, is the way I heard the story. Each time, Rey changed the name of the project, shielded his employees from the political issues, and kept them focused. Eventually they solved the technical problems and created the RAMAC, the first random access disk drive. With the success of his project Rey influenced IBM to start a new division called Advanced Systems Development Division (ASDD) based on his ideas and philosophy."

"And his philosophy?" I asked.

"To have a place for people to work on new ideas for the future," Bob informed me. "Rey wanted to hire smart engineers and programmers, give them a good working environment with good support facilities, and let the innovation come from them. ASDD has an excellent model shop where we can build any specialized mechanical or electrical hardware for a project. Also there is an excellent technical library that started when he first arrived in the 1950s and continues to be enhanced. In fact, many of the engineers and model builders from that project work at ASDD today, including the head librarian."

"You're saying the ideas come from the employees. How does that work?" I asked, becoming more and more interested.

"If you have an idea about how computers can be used in a certain area, then you can propose it to the management and receive funding for staff and equipment. This seemed to work well in the beginning but I'm starting to see some changes. In particular, it appears that the project with the flashiest presentation is the one that receives the funding. More and more time is devoted to preparing the sales pitch for the project, which limits the time for doing the actual work. But still," he concluded, "a lot of good work is getting done. There are excellent people and the projects are dynamic. It's a great place to work."

I thanked him for his time and his candidness.

When I drove over to ASDD for my interview, I drove west from the IBM Cottle Road site, toward Los Gatos, along Blossom Hill Road near the foothills at the south end of Santa Clara Valley. Blossom Hill Road is so named because this valley was once covered in orchards and families would drive up on this rise to look out over the blossoms each spring. The ASDD building was nestled against the foothills on Guadalupe Mines Road. It was an innovative design: a simple, one story building constructed of redwood and glass. Walking from the visitor's parking lot up the few steps into the main lobby, I looked across to an interior, window-lined courtyard with a fountain. A brass plaque on the fountain quoted Rey Johnson:

"Your first responsibility is to answer the questions of your colleagues."

Walking down the wide corridor of the main hall, I turned into a smaller hall and a private office for my interview. This office had a window overlooking another interior courtyard. I learned that the building was designed and constructed to facilitate moving the walls to rearrange the office space. But the design made the walls look permanent. The walls were white, floor to ceiling, five-foot sections with borders of redwood molding. The office space could be rearranged by unscrewing the molding to reveal the hidden framework. The wall sections were repositioned within the underlying framework and the molding was reinstalled. Nothing looked temporary but there was flexibility to redesign the space as needed. A manager had a 10'x10' office. Two people shared a 10'x15' office. All of the offices had windows that looked outside or onto an interior courtyard. After the various offices I had occupied on a manufacturing floor, in an old farmhouse, and in temporary trailers, I was very impressed with this facility. "It would be very difficult to work somewhere else after working here," I thought.

The project with the opening for a programmer was the Library Management System (LMS). The librarian, Marjorie Griffin, who had worked with Rey Johnson since the early days in downtown San Jose, was the guiding light of this project to automate libraries. Watching the development of computers, she envisioned how they could help run her technical library and finally she convinced ASDD to start a project and use her library as a model.

I interviewed with Bob Alexander, the applications designer for the LMS.

"We're not just looking at Marjorie's library but at the requirements for large institutional libraries like university libraries and public libraries. We want to put all the functions of a library online with an interactive interface," he told me.

He went on to tell me that right now, in the mid-1960s, as computers become increasingly available, the different library managers at universities or public libraries were ordering computers to solve a particular departmental problem. Perhaps they wanted to automate the ordering process, or the circulation process. But these systems were not designed to inter-connect to one another since they were looking at the library in a piecemeal fashion and not as an integrated whole. The LMS project was designed to integrate all the processes in a library: ordering, receiving, cataloging, indexing, searching, and circulating.

"We have the file system designed and loaded with all the information from the index cards for the books in Marjorie's library," he continued. "Now we're ready to design and implement the other functions: ordering, receiving, cataloging, etc. This is where you come in. We need a programmer to implement these functions. Do you want the job?"

I had reservations. At first glance, it seemed like another example of a large project trying to do everything for everyone. But this project had several advantages. For one thing, they were actually writing programs and building the system. For another, the library and the librarians were located right in the same building and we could ask them questions about how the system should work. In addition, there were only about five programmers working on the project so there were fewer people to coordinate with. I decided to take the job and started exactly one month after I had filed my Request for Transfer.

Thus began a most productive and satisfying job assignment. Bob Martin was the lead programmer on the project. I was in the unusual situation where he would give me programming assignments during the day for the LMS project, and I would give him programming assignments for the PL/I class I was teaching after work.

Bob explained the design of the file system. All the library data for each book, each author, every subject, and every publisher was stored in computerized records on a magnetic disk storage device: a stack of magnetic disks called a disk pack. At this time disk storage was still very expensive and it was not foreseen how the price would drop over the years. The file design minimized the use of disk storage and eliminated redundant data. He repeatedly said that one extra byte of data per book would amount to a million extra bytes of data in a million-volume library. The attention to saving disk space was a guiding factor[13].

The data for each book was stored as an individual record in the document file and assigned a unique five-byte document identifier, or pointer. This pointer consisted of the record number (the location of the record on the disk) and an offset into the record. With this five-byte document pointer, we could quickly read the data from the external disk and reference all the information about a book. When a new book was added to the library it was added sequentially to this file and assigned a new document pointer.

The author index (a list of all the authors in the library) was stored in a separate file containing records for each author name followed by a list of document pointers to the books written by that author. This file was in alphabetical order and a new author was inserted alphabetically and assigned a unique author pointer (record number and offset). In a similar manner there were title, publisher, and subject index files.

The record for a specific book mostly contained a list of pointers to other records: typically pointers to one or more authors, a pointer to the title, a pointer to the publisher, and a list of pointers to the subjects. The routines that retrieved the information about a book followed these pointers, reading the records off the disk, and extracting the author, title, publisher, and subject details.

With the file system designed, implemented and loaded with real data, we were soon displaying the results of simple searches on the IBM 2260 display terminal. This was the same display terminal that I had used as a simulator in the purchasing project but now there was real data in a file system driving the display. The 2260 allowed for 12 lines of 80 characters each. There was one line, at the bottom, to accept input from the terminal.

To search for a book the librarian first selected an index (author, title, subject, or publisher). If searching by author, for example, they then typed the first few letters of the author's name. The program accessed the author index and displayed the four items that fell alphabetically before and after their entry. The librarian could select a specific author by typing its corresponding number on the input line. Or they could type "F" or "B" to scroll forward or backward through the list of authors.

Bob Martin explained the programming environment. The programming language was IBM System/360 Assembler Language. The code was written in 4K blocks (4096 bytes of instructions), and an experimental multitasking monitor managed task switching by swapping the blocks in and out of memory. The experimental multitasking monitor was stored on one of the removable disk packs. Whenever we had dedicated computer time for testing, we mounted this disk pack and booted up the operating system with our multitasking monitor that drove the 2260 display terminals for the library project. All the library data files were stored on another disk pack that was also up and running.

I enjoyed writing in Assembler language and fitting all my instructions within a 4K block or starting another block that I could call as a subroutine. I also enjoyed working with the librarians. I taught them the new functions and features as they were developed. The librarians were eager to use the new system and very patient with the "crashes" that inevitably occurred with any newly developing system. They were particularly good about describing what they were doing when everything quit and that made it easier to reproduce the problem and fix it.

We had a great team working on the project. Bob Alexander was the LMS overall manager. Marjorie Griffin was the manager of the library. Stratton and Caryl McAllister were a husband and wife team at ASDD. He worked on the technical aspects of the multitasking monitor; she was knowledgeable about the library requirements. Bob Martin was the technical lead. Jack Christensen worked on the file system. Alice McMullen programmed anything and everything. Vi Ma and Cay Rafferty were librarians.

John Bell and I worked on the design and implementation of the ordering, receiving, and cataloging functions. When we were designing these functions, we met for a week or so in the small conference room next to the office of the lab manager, Lou Stevens. We mapped out how these functions would interrelate with each other and the file system. We specified routines and their interfaces. In this office I sat across from a painting of a man sitting in a rowing shell on a peaceful stream lined with trees. This was a welcomed working environment to design the programs and their interfaces: a small, quiet, light-filled conference room; only two people working out the ideas; a lovely painting on the wall and no one smoking.

We wanted to capture the information about a book only once and eliminate the duplicate typing that always led to the possibility of errors. Currently the librarians typed this information over and over again: on the purchase order and on the multitude of index cards for the card catalog.

Again, I was working on designing an ordering system to satisfy multiple requirements. But this was not as abstract as the purchasing project in the Manufacturing Division. Now there was a library down the hall and librarians who wanted to use the system to order new publications. We designed ordering screens for the 2260 with an interface to the existing file system. When ordering a book the librarian would type the author's name or even just a few letters of the author's name. Our programs used these few keystrokes to interface to the file system and display the existing author names. If the author's name already existed in the file system, the librarian could select it from the list and eliminate the situation where the same author is listed under multiple spellings. If it did not exist, we switched to a screen where the librarian entered the complete author name and our routine added the name to the author index. The same process was repeated for additional authors and for the title and publisher. By the time the book was ordered, most of the information for cataloging was already captured. We set the status of the new book to "on order." When the book arrived the librarian found the existing book information by any of the authors or titles previously entered. The book status was then changed to "received" and additional cataloging information (subjects and location) was added. The book was then available for circulation.

We had a subroutine interface for input and output to and from the 2260 display terminal. The calling routine would pass this subroutine a screen of data to be written on the display and a data field to hold the response typed by the librarian. Often the librarian typed a number to select an option from the screen. For instance, if they were entering a new order they would first select from a list of functions the number that corresponded to "new order" on the screen. The next screen would ask if they wanted to enter the author or title, the next screen would ask for the author or title name, the next screen would display the current authors or titles from the file system and ask them to choose an existing or enter a new one.

To make this process more efficient, we invented something we called "command chaining." This allowed the librarians, who could anticipate the next screen, to key in the responses to the subsequent screens all at once. The answers were separated by a slash "/." As the librarians became used to the system they could answer ahead of time the questions they knew would be asked on the next few screens.

This was all handled by the input/output (I/O) subroutine which would collect the input from the 2260, and scan for the "/" that separated the responses. It returned the first response to the calling routine and saved the rest of the responses. The next time the I/O routine was called it checked to see if it already had the response and, if so, returned it to the calling routine without displaying anything on the 2260. The calling routine did not know if the response came from the previously saved data in the command chain or from the newly typed entry at the display terminal, but the calling routine could override the command chain by setting a flag specifying that it really wanted the information displayed on the display terminal and reviewed by the librarian. If the flag was set, the I/O routine erased the rest of the command chain and displayed the screen data on the 2260. This was usually done when something had to be confirmed visually by the librarian before it was updated in the file system.

Command chaining was self-taught and very popular with the librarians. As they became more familiar with the system, they knew what would be on the next screen, since it was determined by their response to the current screen, so they typed in the next response. I remember Cay showing me her command line for ordering a book where she entered 12 or 14 answers ahead of time. She was very proud.

One by one we implemented the ordering, receiving, and cataloging functions. One by one we taught the librarians how to use these functions. Step by step the library functions were being automated into one integrated system. There were still more functions to design and implement. Periodicals had different requirements from books. Circulation had not been addressed yet.

In the midst of this designing, programming, debugging, testing, and teaching the librarians, we were also giving demonstrations of the system to upper management and outside visitors. The librarians from Stanford University were our guests one afternoon and their eyes sparkled in recognition of the advantages of the online, integrated library system we presented. The pressure to demonstrate the system and renew our funding occurred on a regular basis. As Bob Martin told me before I arrived, a lot of time and effort was spent preparing a polished sales presentation of our project in order to compete with the other projects for funding.

Once, I gave a demonstration to the IBM Chief Scientist. I do not remember the name of this man, but I remember the experience. I was in a 10'x10' office sitting in front of a 2260 display terminal describing how the Library Management System (LMS) worked. Also in the office were my manager, his manager, and the lab manager. There may have even been an IBM Vice-President. The ASDD division reported to the IBM top management and I think there were only five levels of management between the president, Thomas Watson, Jr., and me.

The Chief Scientist sat to my left. I began my demonstration of the file system, the searching, the ordering, and the command chaining features. I had finished only half of my first explanation when he interrupted me to say "Go on." This happened several times in a row and I must have had a startled expression on my face with each interruption. He then paused to say that he did this to everyone and to please continue. I realized that he caught on very quickly to each idea and he did not need further explanation. He was very bright and rapidly picked up one concept after another. At the end I could only hope that he did come away with a clear picture of the system.

I started working on an advanced searching function. Currently we asked the user to select one of the indexes into the file system—book title, author, or subject—and enter a keyword. I designed and implemented a Boolean search where you could enter several keywords, an author and a subject for example, in order to locate an item in the file system more quickly. This Boolean search was very primitive and I wished for something more sophisticated, but I did not have the vision to design it. Today's search engines[14], like the one in Google[15], exceed my wildest imagination.

Now we faced the problem of backup and recovery if the system went down in the middle of adding a new book. We hired another programmer and this was his main focus. He designed an innovative solution for recovering the database in case of a system crash. This was particularly important because adding a book to the database involved updating pointers in multiple index files. All the "writes" needed to take place to maintain the integrity of the file system. If the system crashed before it was complete then the database needed to be reset to the prior condition.

As we finished the basic functions, we opened the system for general use by the ASDD scientists and engineers, and card catalog index cards became obsolete. Progress was being made on a daily and weekly basis.

Then the Library Management System project *was cancelled!* It was mid-1969 and I had been on the project for over a year. I remember my shock when I learned this. It was too unbelievable to comprehend. We were not done. There were many more functions to design and implement. I was not one to keep track of the daily shifts in the IBM internal political winds. In fact, about a year earlier, a colleague noted this and commented to me, "You may sleep better each night because you're not fretting over the internal politics, but you may also be in for a rude awakening someday."

This was that rude awakening. The political winds had shifted and we lost our funding. I have vague memories that we focused on submitting the unique ideas in LMS for patents. And Marjorie Griffin, the head librarian, campaigned and won the right to keep LMS running in her library.

LMS had received some funding from a public source outside of IBM. Whatever this source was it meant that the programs we had designed and implemented were in the public domain. Caryl and Stratton McAllister were committed to continuing this work and eventually left IBM to hire on to IBM Germany, which was structurally a different company. They picked up the code from the public domain and continued to develop the Library Management System under a different name and in a different country. They worked diligently at IBM Germany in cooperation with German libraries. In 1973, when I traveled to Germany on a vacation, I visited the McAllisters and also visited the library at Dortmund University where it was installed. For years and years the McAllisters continued to build this system and install it in European universities.

Meanwhile I was at a loss. I had been so enthusiastic and dedicated to this exciting and worthwhile project. The idea of using computers to automate libraries appealed to my sense of how computers could provide information at our fingertips. I had worked with talented people in a great environment. But now I was stunned by the decision to cancel the project and I was stopped in my tracks.

1969
Recycling Computer Paper

While we were writing programs for the Library Management System, outside major events were impacting IBM and us. In 1969 the U.S. Department of Justice issued an antitrust suit against IBM for monopolistic practices. As employees we were told to save all documents, regardless, in case they were needed for the suit. That meant we saved every computer listing, and a stack was growing in our office.

I shared an office with Alice McMullen. About fifteen years older than I, a graduate of the University of California at Berkeley in math, she was an experienced programmer. We developed our programs, assembled and debugged them in a batch mode, submitting our jobs and picking up the listings from the computer lab down the hall. Alice checked and rechecked the logic of her code before submitting it such that she often received error free listings on the first try. I, on the other hand, had more of a tendency to let the assembler catch my errors. This is similar to how today, when using a word processor, we have a tendency to let the spell checker catch our spelling errors. But in this case the computer printed a listing of the errors.

I stepped through the logic of my code more carefully but still I watched as the stack of computer listings accumulated in our office. As the months went by I imagined the warehouses all over the country that were storing these IBM documents for the government. I became aware that this would be an excellent source for recycling paper when the suit was over. It was all collected and when it was not needed anymore the paper could be recycled, especially the computer paper. I knew a bit about recycling newspaper from when my brothers participated in Boy Scout paper drives. I knew that newsprint was made with long wood fibers, to withstand the high speeds of the printing presses, and could be recycled into other paper products. I thought that the computer paper would be another good source for recycling. When guidelines came down from the legal department saying that we no longer had to save every computer listing, I decided to act on my recycling idea.

IBM had a suggestion program that rewarded an employee with a percentage of any savings created by the implementation of their suggestion. So I submitted a suggestion for recycling computer paper and waited for my response. The letter I received back from the Suggestion Department declined my suggestion, saying it was not feasible. I was angry. It did not seem like they had really investigated the idea but just denied it out-of-hand so I sat down to write a vitriolic response to the Suggestion Department describing how incompetent they were in handling my suggestion.

In the midst of composing this letter I spoke to an engineering friend and told him how upset I was with the Suggestion Department. I described the letter I was writing.

He looked at me and said, "Do you want to have a fight with the Suggestion Department or do you want IBM to recycle computer paper?"

I replied, "I want IBM to recycle computer paper."

Then he coached me by saying, "You know the Facilities Manager of our location, George Ferguson. Go and share your idea with him. He can implement it."

I took this advice. I talked with George and shared the information about local vendors who would buy the paper for recycling. He agreed to look into it and subsequently acted on it. Within weeks our IBM location, the Los Gatos ASDD Lab, was recycling computer paper. After this had been going on for a few months, George asked me what I wanted to do with the money they were receiving for selling the recycled paper. I, of course, said they could give it to me, but that was just in jest. I suggested the money be donated to the Sempervirens Fund[16], an organization dedicated to preserving redwood forests, in particular the redwood forest in the nearby Santa Cruz Mountains.[17] With this experience, I learned the valuable lesson of the difference between complaining and taking action. I was about to expend energy complaining about the Suggestion Department. I could certainly tell the story about their ineffectiveness to anyone who would listen, but I was redirected to take positive action to accomplish my goal. I have had opportunities to learn this lesson repeatedly. If I am able to catch myself focusing on complaining, then I remember this incident and shift my thinking to look for other ways to take action and accomplish my goal.

Meanwhile, George Ferguson took my idea further. He regularly attended meetings with Facilities Managers from different IBM sites, and he shared how Los Gatos ASDD was recycling computer paper. Soon the San Jose site, the Boulder site, and the Poughkeepsie site were also recycling. I never received an award from the Suggestion Department, but IBM started recycling computer paper and that was my goal. I did receive an informal award when the director of the ASDD Lab, Lou Stevens, presented me with $500 in appreciation of my efforts.

I was also acknowledged in another way. IBM's *Think* magazine published an article in June 1971 about how I started the program to recycle computer paper. It featured a photo of me standing in front of stacks and stacks of computer listings. They titled the article "The Hitchcock Formula," described my interest in the environment, and indicated how many trees were saved by each ton of paper recycled. They didn't get this formula from me, but somehow it made a good focus for their story. I have a framed copy of this article from *Think* magazine hanging on the wall in my home today.

1970-1973
New Ideas

When the Library Management Project ended and we finished writing and submitting our patents, it was early 1970 and I started looking at going back to school. I thought about getting a Master's degree in mathematics or computer science, since now there were universities where I could study advanced computer science. As I pondered the possibility of returning to school however, I became aware of another desire in me. Instead of going deeper into one field of study I wanted to go more broadly into a wider range of studies. I was interested in areas that I had not explored before.

I decided to take the summer off and attend summer school at the University of California at Berkeley. I applied for and received a three-month personal leave of absence from IBM for the summer of 1970. I put my belongings in storage, moved from the house I shared with Cathy Jones, and took a few things with me to Berkeley, where I rented a room near the university. I walked over to the campus and sat in the sunshine watching the other students on their way to and from class. I had just left behind all my previous obligations.

Even with classes I quickly realized that I did not like my days to be so unstructured. So I went to the local radio station and volunteered as a receptionist from 4 to 6 p.m. every weekday. My classes were in anthropology, sociology, Greek dancing, and pottery. The sociology class addressed how minority groups change societies by introducing new ideas that work their way into the accepted norms. My budding awareness of social justice led me to attend trials to see our justice system at work. Because I was volunteering at the radio station, I asked and received permission to produce a radio interview program illuminating the conditions in our jail system. My interest in art led me to visit local art galleries and exhibitions. I attended plays and went to the Greek restaurants in the evening to join my classmates in Greek dancing. I went camping. I drove to Seattle and visited family. I visited the University of California library and saw their efforts to automate their library. I was exploring.

All too soon it was September and my three-month leave of absence was over. I had not imagined how this experience would change me. During the summer I had not actively looked for other job opportunities. Unwilling to quit IBM without another job, now, by default, I was returning to my job at IBM. I moved back to the Palo Alto area and found a place to live with new roommates in Atherton.

With all my exploring of new directions, I found it very difficult to re-compartmentalize myself into the structure of the IBM workday. Something deep inside me would not let me put my foot back on the path of my IBM career. I became very depressed and soon I was unable to go to work. The shock and shame of not being able to function completely dominated my attention, and I lost sight that there might have been some fundamental questions about the meaning of life that I had begun to explore. Was life about going to school, graduating, getting a job, earning a good income and then what? I was not against marriage and I certainly imagined that I would have a family with children, but even though I had male companions for my hiking and skiing adventures, whenever one of them became more interested in me, I found myself backing away and disappearing from the relationship.

This depression lasted several months and I was on an IBM medical leave of absence while I received counseling. My counselor felt that I was mourning the death of my mother, somehow postponed in the intervening years. Raised to focus on productivity, my emotions were more of a mystery to me. I had no idea that they could knock me off my feet in such a dramatic way. Slowly I recovered and returned to work at IBM ASDD in Los Gatos. My colleagues were very sympathetic and supportive of me. One recommended that I have a long talk with his wife. Another said I would feel much better if I went for a walk on the beach. I realized that they were telling me what worked for them when they were experiencing a difficult time, but I knew that I needed to find what worked for me.

The summer of 1971, while working full time, I went every weekend to the Sierra on backpacking trips where the beauty of the mountains nourished me. The next spring I traveled to the Grand Canyon for a rafting trip on the Colorado River. Perhaps I had concluded, again by default, that earning a good living and being able to take vacations to see this fabulous world was what life was all about. But two weeks of vacation time per year never seemed satisfying enough.

I still was seeking a new direction and I had this desire to learn. I applied and was accepted to a Stanford graduate program in Operations Research[18]. I attended one quarter in the fall and found that the course work did not interest me.

My explorations led to my discovery of a couple of innovative projects near Stanford University. I visited Rey Johnson at his private research lab in Palo Alto. Rey, now retired from IBM, was exploring ideas on how to improve literacy. He invented and demonstrated a handheld device to "read" a small disk inserted into the page of a book. When you placed the handheld device over the disk it read, out loud, the corresponding text. It was simple enough that a child could use it. This technology was referred to as a micro-phonograph and was subsequently used by Fisher Price in the "Talk to Me Books."

When I visited the Stanford Research Institute in Menlo Park, I met inventor Doug Engelbart[19] and saw an early demonstration of the computer mouse[20] he invented to solve the challenges of human-computer interaction. Instead of typing on the keyboard to select an option on the display he demonstrated pointing to it with the mouse. I was fascinated by this way of communicating to a computer but did not see it in actual use for many years.

Meanwhile, in my day-to-day work life at ASDD in 1971, I worked on an Office Automation project called OASIS. We were working with ideas on how computers could be used to make office work more efficient. As part of this project, in order to understand the requirements, I visited two Internal Revenue Service Offices, one in Washington D.C. and one in a Midwestern state. The director of one facility gave me a tour and described how they processed the returns. He had designed a very efficient processing system where the tax returns flowed from one person (for data entry) to the next (for verification) like a manufacturing assembly line. I was writing specifications and documentation for the OASIS Project, not computer programs. We, or at least I, did not envision transmitting tax returns electronically and processing the data without the need for data entry. Although Emil Hopner, a colleague at ASDD originally from Switzerland with eyes that twinkled, often shared his ideas about sending documents electronically, thereby eliminating the need for the post office. Still I did not connect the dots and realize that this could be a way of sending tax returns.

Ernie Nassimbene[21], also at ASDD, worked on the Universal Product Code (UPC), the barcode that can be scanned. I remember hearing that it was his ideas that led to the breakthrough that allowed the barcode to be scanned forward, backwards, and sideways but still yield the same result. To demonstrate the usability of the barcode, ASDD started a pilot project with the Yellow Freight Company to show how to track the shipment of boxes using barcodes and a scanner. I had friends who worked on this project and who shared their excitement building and demonstrating this new capability. This is now the common way of tracking shipments.

The Cash Issuing Terminal, now called automatic teller machine (ATM), was developed at ASDD. Alice McMullen, my officemate on the LMS project, worked on writing the microcode[22] (hardware-level instructions) for the early devices. At lunch she would tell us about the glitches of debugging the code to dispense twenty-dollar bills. This project led to an IBM product, the IBM 3614[23], the first automated teller machine, and Alice transferred with the project to Charlotte, North Carolina, where she became one of the technical managers.

The ASDD environment was dynamic, and lunchtime conversations were filled with ideas about new possible projects. Here I first began to hear ideas about desktop computing or personal computers. One colleague lamented that IBM management only saw software as a way to sell hardware. She said that management did not see the possibility of a profitable business based on selling software. This was prophetic because just a couple of years later IBM went outside the company for the operating system for their personal computer. The young man who provided the operating system, Bill Gates, went on to create the Microsoft company based on building and marketing software.

I participated in testing a bill-pay-by-phone experimental project. This project modeled the steps for paying bills using a telephone. I dialed a phone number, listened to the electronically generated prompts, and selected the options by entering the numbers on the push-button phone. In this way I selected and paid utility bills, mortgage payments, and rent. When I completed the procedure, I was asked my opinion about the usability of the system. I was not too enthusiastic about the process. It was an intriguing idea overall, but I did not have many bills to pay and it was easy enough to just write checks and mail them. My response was similar to my reaction when I first encountered push-button phones when they were introduced at the 1962 Seattle Worlds Fair.

Placed side-by-side with a rotary dial[24] phone, we were invited to try them both and see which was faster. I was not overly impressed with the push-button phone at the time. Now, of course, push-button phones are the norm and I am very pleased with the convenience of the online banking and bill pay facilities I use.

One new device really did impress me, however, when in the early 1970s I first saw a thin, flexible eight-inch square floppy disk[25]. I immediately saw the value in a small, portable, magnetic data storage device. In the library project we used disk packs, a stack of magnetically coated disk platters, to store the library data. The floppy disk contained the initial commands for booting[26] up an external piece of electronic equipment. It was not for our project but I was intrigued by the possibility of storing data on a portable device and I kept this floppy disk on my desk as a reminder of this new capability. Now we have portable flash drives[27], the size of a thumb, which hold large quantities of data.

As I continued to look around for new learning opportunities, I applied for and was accepted to the IBM Systems Research Institute. This institute was like a graduate school program available to IBM programmers and engineers. Held in New York City, in a building across the street from the United Nations, the program was three months long and the classes were held every day from 9 a.m. to 6 p.m. I lived in New York City from September to December in 1972, all expenses paid, in a hotel on the corner of 34th and Broadway. Mornings I walked across town, stopping first at a restaurant for breakfast, to attend classes—seven lectures a day and an educational movie at noon. Evenings I went to dinner and to performances—plays, operas, symphonies and ballets. It was an intellectually and culturally stimulating experience.

My favorite class was Queueing Theory[28]. Imagine the lines (queues) at a bank, post office, escalator, or grocery store. You immediately scan these lines and mentally choose the optimal one for yourself. Inside a complicated computer operating system similar choices need to be programmed to optimize the processing. During one memorable class the instructor stood at the blackboard illustrating algorithms and solving queuing equations, doing most of the mathematical calculations rapidly in his head. I was intent on following his explanation and rapid-fire calculations when, chalk in hand, he suddenly remember that he had just bought a brand new Hewlett-Packard handheld calculator. It was the fall of 1972 and HP had just announced the HP-35[29]. He stopped in the middle of doing the next calculation, turned, walked to his desk, reached down to pickup his large briefcase, opened his briefcase, took out the box that held the new calculator, took the calculator out of the box, turned on the calculator, and entered in the two numbers he was about to multiply. He wrote the answer on the board, turned off the calculator, put it back in its box, put the box back in the briefcase, closed the briefcase, put it back on the floor, and returned to the blackboard. Then he continued his presentation doing all the rest of the calculations in his head. Seeing this first use of the HP calculator, I saw it as a cumbersome tool for doing calculations that the instructor could do more quickly in his head. But the ability and pride of doing calculations in one's head has now been lost with the prevalence of calculators.

One result of the Queuing Theory class with all the discussion of single servers, multiple servers, single or multiple queues, and service capacity was that I started looking at the world from the view of queuing theory. For instance, I chuckled as class let out and a hundred students headed for the stairs that could not serve that quantity of people in a timely manner, forming a queue of students at the top of the steps. It was an exciting learning environment and I was constantly exploring new ideas.

When I returned to ASDD I felt that, with all the new experiences, I must have been away for longer than three months. But at ASDD it seemed as if time had stood still and nothing had changed. I wondered how I could bring back some of what I had experienced in New York to my work place. Then I remembered the educational movies shown at noon in New York, and soon I initiated a noontime movie series at ASDD. I ordered the films from the UC Berkeley film lending library and showed them in the auditorium once a week.

The first film I showed was a short animated film called *Why Man Creates*.[30] In one segment of the film a cartoon character, a snail in a shell, sticks his head out of his shell and says, "Did you ever stop to think that radical ideas threaten institutions, then become institutions that are threatened by radical ideas?"

The other character responds with, "No."

The first character pulls his head back into his shell and mumbles, "Oh, I thought I had something there."[31] I know from personal experience that a person putting out a new idea may well retract it when the current norm does not see its value.

1971
Carpooling Program

In 1971, I shared a house in Atherton, California with three women. Each morning I would leave early, in my green MGB GT sports car, and drive through the tree-lined, back streets to Stanford University. There I joined a recent graduate student and we carpooled the rest of the way to IBM's ASDD Lab in Los Gatos. In the foothills behind Stanford we merged onto Highway 280. In summer the hills were golden brown with the occasional green of a live oak tree. In mid-winter the hills were a lovely green with yellow Acacia shrubs blooming. The road curved gently between these hills then emerged from the hills to cross the Santa Clara Valley. We could see the expanse of homes and shopping centers that covered the valley.

In the 1950s this valley was called "Valley of Heart's Delight" because it was covered in orchards whose fruit was shipped all over the world. Now the valley had a new name: "Silicon Valley" because of the silicon used to make high-tech computer integrated circuits.

The freeway ended in the middle of the valley and we merged southbound on Highway 17. Within an exit or two we left the freeway and commuted on city streets stopping for red lights, passing shopping centers, schools, and homes. Eventually, after about an hour of driving, we came to Guadalupe Mines Road and the site of the modern redwood and glass building for the ASDD Lab.

During this commute I realized how many cars were on the road with only one person per car. I thought people could share rides if they only knew other people who lived near them and were going the same way. I figured out how to write a computer program to match people coming from the same area and going to IBM. It involved putting their name and home location (specified as the coordinates from a city map) on a punched card. The cards would be sorted and then printed to give each person a list of people from their area. I wrote the program and tested it.

I went to the IBM Personnel Department[32] to offer this as a service to the employees. I met with the personnel manager in his office. It was an office just big enough for his desk, facing the door, and two visitor chairs. I sat down.

"I have written a computer program to match people by where they live so they can form carpools to come to work," I said by way of introduction.

But the personnel manager wasn't interested. "The way people get to and from work is their responsibility not IBM's," he said dismissively.

I was flustered. I did not expect to be met with this opposition to what I considered a contribution. What could I say? "But IBM is subsidizing people arriving in individual cars because IBM is paying a huge amount of money for parking lots."

He sat across from me and reached for a cigarette. Perhaps he was uncomfortable and had no response for my, obviously true, observation.

Since he was not going to be any help with promoting the carpool idea, I said, "Maybe I could stand out in the parking lot and give out information sheets to people to see how many would be interested in carpooling."

His hand stopped in mid-air with the lit match aiming at his cigarette. He looked up, directly into my eyes. "That would not be a good idea," he said with a chilling firmness.

It was strong enough to stop me from further discussion and I left his office. I did not realize at the moment what he was saying. Later I understood. I had touched on a very sensitive nerve. Any action that looked like organizing employees would seem like an effort to unionize IBM. My comment about handing out questionnaires to employees was too close to organizing for him to be comfortable.

I returned to my office and put the computer program—a stack of computer cards—on the corner of my desk. I had no place to file it and I wanted it to stay in my awareness. For months and months it sat on my desk, always reminding me of what I was trying to accomplish. Two years later, when the 1973 oil embargo[33] started and gas prices soared and people had to wait in long lines to purchase fuel, I received a call from the personnel manager asking about my program to match people for carpooling. That is when IBM implemented my carpooling program. A map was posted on the employee's bulletin board with the information about how to participate. Each person submitted a card that specified the area on the map where they lived, and they were matched with others from the same area. I never knew how successful it was in terms of how many people were matched or how many carpools were formed. But for many years I continued to see the map posted on the employee's bulletin board.

1974
Turning Point

One day, in early 1974, all the ASDD employees were called into the cafeteria for a meeting and IBM management announced that the division was terminated. I was not surprised because I could see that ASDD no longer functioned according to its original mission. No longer were ideas initiated by the engineers and programmers, instead a more structured management dictated the projects and schedules. No longer were we looking out seven years into the future. This announcement terminated ASDD officially, but as a working environment it had already disappeared. We were told that we would all be reassigned to existing projects in the Systems Development Division (SDD). It took months to realize this transition from ASDD to SDD as we wrapped up and documented our current work as best we could. I co-authored a report, with another woman, documenting the status of our current project.

ASDD had been a unique environment in IBM with a focus on future uses of computers. Now the small redwood and glass building on Guadalupe Mines Road contained a new set of managers reporting to SDD whose mission was to develop and ship products in the near term. Only the model shop survived in the building with its talented model builders who provided support for projects across division boundaries for a number of years.

Marjorie Griffin had the disheartening task of dismantling the technical library that she had built over the last twenty years. She did that with all the grace of her British Columbia background and soon retired. Some of the contents of that library migrated to the IBM San Jose Research Division library where Vi Ma soon transferred and continued to work as the head librarian for many years. Many of the engineers and computer scientists from ASDD went on to work at the IBM San Jose Research Lab. Eventually I did also, but via a circuitous path.

When ASDD was cancelled I was twenty-nine years old, restless, and full of questions. What was my direction? Was I just going to keep working at IBM? Over the last couple of years none of my projects lasted very long or produced tangible results. Nothing had captured my imagination and heart like the library project. Some of my friends had already left the Los Gatos Lab: one to teach at a junior college; one to start a completely different career in stained glass; one on temporary assignment with IBM in England; several to other opportunities in IBM. As I struggled to find my place in this different IBM division, I interviewed with several projects, looking for an assignment. Soon I found a project called Future Systems (FS). Most of the SDD work was done at the IBM main site on Cottle Road, but this project was being done in Palo Alto, only a mile or so from my home. This would eliminate my 45-minute commute and I could bike to work. I hoped I was making the right decision as I told the manager I would accept the job when I finished document-ing my current work.

Still, I was restless for change, yet not sure where I wanted to go, or how to get there. Then, one fairly normal workday as I was finishing up at ASDD, I attended a late morning seminar. I walked into the auditorium and took a seat. Jacqueline Grennan Wexler[34], the president of Hunter College in New York City, was the speaker. She was talking about how so many young people want change, big change, and radical change. This was the early '70s with unrest and protests on the campuses. Then she spoke about the realistic, steady path of change, growth, and progress.

I sat there as her presentation flowed over me. Here was someone in a position of authority, a woman, speaking on the same things I had been struggling with: how change occurs for people, corporations, and societies.

I knew that there was a luncheon following the presenta-tion, and I knew Marjorie Griffin had arranged for the speak-er and the luncheon.

"Marjorie!" I said as I ran up to her. "I want to come to the luncheon."

Marjorie looked at her guest list and shook her head. "I am sorry, Kathy. All the places are taken."

I turned and walked away, still excited by all the ideas that had been expressed but disappointed to not be able to attend the luncheon. I knew some of the people on the guest list. The retired founder of our laboratory, Rey Johnson, was attending with his wife. I slowly walked back up through the auditorium, immersed in my thoughts, when a moment later Marjorie stopped me.

"Rey's wife couldn't make it," she said. "You can have her place at the luncheon."

This all happened so fast that I could barely catch my breath. The next thing I knew I was seated at a long table with white tablecloth and place settings for twenty people. I looked around to locate the speaker. She was off to my right, down at the other end of the table and too far away for me to be able to talk with her personally. I could just barely hear some of her conversation, and I wanted to know so much more about what she had to say.

I was introduced to the man sitting on my left. He was an IBM vice-president. My first comment to him was: "How do corporations change if they keep promoting into management people who think the same way as the current managers?"

To his credit he responded by asking: "What would you like to see changed?" This was not going to be an abstract conversation about change. He directed it immediately to the practical.

"Well," I said, "I've written a computer program to match people so they can carpool to work. When I went to the personnel department to see if we could offer this program to the employees, I was told that the way people get to and from work was the employee's responsibility, not the company's responsibility."

He sidestepped me once again when he asked, "Do you know about the work Dr. Pat Mantey is doing in the San Jose Research Division? It's a project involving geographic database problems."

"No, I don't."

"You should go talk to him," he said, "I'll call him and let him know to expect you."

The result of this luncheon was an appointment the next day with Dr. Mantey. Here I learned about the ideas they were exploring to solve a class of problems that require geographical data. They were looking at how to organize the data to facilitate searches based on location, path, and direction. He felt that my ideas of matching people for carpools was exactly the type of geographical problem they were addressing. Did I want to come and spend a summer internship working in his department?

Yes, of course I did, yet I had just accepted a job in Palo Alto with the FS project. But something happened in that moment: I became very clear and I determined my own path. I would take the internship position and delay going to the new department for a few months.

I did not ask permission from my manager; instead, the next day I told him my plan for the summer internship and consequently the delay in the transfer to Palo Alto. I ended the conversation by saying that the funding issues needed to be resolved but I was sure that he could work them out. "After all," I thought, "funding and head count are the domains of management." Indeed he worked out a creative solution where my salary was split three ways with one part paid by his department, one part paid by San Jose Research, and one part paid by the FS project.

That led to a summer working on the GADS project in San Jose Research. GADS stood for Geographical Access

Data Systems. This was very early research into storing and retrieving geographical data. Information files were usually organized sequentially, either in alphabetical or numeric order, to allow ease of accessing the data. Geographical data needs to be organized based on what is nearby in order to quickly determine a route from one place to the next or to determine what is close by. Geographical data is stored as a network of interlinked data points. I redesigned my carpool program to use the GADS data structures to efficiently determine who lived nearby or traveled the same route to work. It was a wonderful summer of engaging work with bright, forward thinking colleagues.

The GADS project was under the Computer Science Department in the IBM Research Division. IBM Research[35], now with eleven worldwide laboratories, had three locations at the time: San Jose, Yorktown Heights[36] in New York and Zurich, Switzerland. San Jose Research began when Rey Johnson set up the IBM West Coast Laboratory in 1952 in downtown San Jose, then it was moved to the IBM Cottle Road site when that location was built.

IBM San Jose Research, located next to the manufacturing and development of disk storage devices, had a focus on projects that could enhance the disk technology both with material science research and with computer science research. Ted Codd[37], the inventor of the relational model[38] for database management, worked here and wrote his 1970 paper on relational databases. Don Chamberlain and Raymond Boyce, who defined SEQUEL[39] (renamed to SQL) as a special-purpose programming language for managing relational data, worked at IBM San Jose Research. John Backus[40], already named an IBM Fellow[41] as the inventor of Fortran[42], worked here as well.

The Research Division had a different system for advancement and rating employees. Whereas I started at IBM as a Junior Programmer and progressed to Associate Programmer then Staff Programmer, the Research Division had Research Staff Members without the distinction of levels. But as a Research Staff Member you were expected to have a PhD and do original research.

When the summer was over my project manager asked me to stay. He was pleased with my work. It was tempting to accept this new offer, but I declined since I had made a commitment to the FS project and had already delayed the start. And another consideration was the pressure from upper management to only employ PhDs in computer science. Still, it was hard to leave San Jose Research because of the exciting project and the stimulating environment.

1974-1977
A Change in Perception

In the fall of 1974 I left San Jose Research and started to work for IBM in Palo Alto on the Future Systems (FS)[43] project. It was another large, ambitious project, still in the design stage, which was going to do everything. It was so nebulous that I could not determine what to do. One IBMer reviewed the FS project and commented, "The avowed aim of all this red tape is to prevent anyone from understanding the whole system; this goal has certainly been achieved."[44] This completely reflected my experience. Months went by and I was still trying to bring the project into focus when someone in upper IBM management had the wisdom to cancel it.

During this time I lived in a small, rental house on Oxford Avenue in Palo Alto and it was a short walk or bike ride to the IBM buildings on Page Mill Road and California Avenue—the best commute I ever had. One day, as I was walking to work, I remember thinking: "It doesn't seem like any of my projects ever result in anything. I work on them for a while and then they are cancelled for some reason. I don't think I should expect the reward of accomplishment down the road for working hard to get something done. I think that I will need to get my reward in each day of work." So I had a short-term perspective for making each day a satisfying day.

One afternoon I walked into a lab where several men were unpacking and setting up a new printer. The printer was not working correctly as each page had a black line across it. I had worked with this type of printer on the GADS project at San Jose Research so I knew that somehow light was getting into the printer and exposing the page causing the black line. I told them that light was exposing the paper but my explanation was ignored as they speculated that the "clunk" sound was causing it. "No," I said, "that's the paper cutter." This printer produced cut sheets of paper using a photographic process, it was a printer designed for graphic drawings or pictures. Ignored again, the men searched for another solution to the problem of the black line. Eventually they discovered that the cover was not completely closed and light was exposing the paper. I left the room discouraged that my explanation had not been acknowledged.

This incident stands in contrast to another experience when, at the end of a lively, afternoon meeting, one of the men expressed his annoyance with me. "It isn't fair. Everyone in the room stops to listen to what you have to say, but it's because you talk so softly that they have to be quiet in order to hear you."

In the fall of 1975 I was selected to attend a Technical Leadership School for IBM in New York. I do not know how I was selected since I did not apply. The week long class was held at an old estate on Long Island. After flying from San Francisco to New York, after renting a car, after driving out to Long Island, it was a late, stormy night when I drove up the curving driveway to the front of the old estate. As a young woman traveling alone under these conditions I was relieved to discover I had found the right place.

All week we had guest speakers. One presentation stands out in my mind because of its profound impact on me. This speaker presented a convincing argument showing how our perception determines what we see and how we form our understanding of the world. Using an experiment with a rotating trapezoid (about the size of a large, rectangular playing card, with one side shorter than the other, mounted on a wire post, rotating around its center), he showed that we initially "saw" it oscillate back and forth, not rotate, because we did not want to give up our perception that it was a rectangle (where the shorter side would never move in front of the longer side). Then he attached a small, red ball to the corner of the trapezoid and again set it rotating on the stand across the room. Viewed with one eye covered, we "saw" the red ball break loose from the trapezoid and "float" through the air to re-attach on the other side. We "saw" this, he said, because we did not want to give up our perception that we were looking at a rectangle (one of the most familiar shapes) and recognize that it was a more complex trapezoid. What we see, he said, is what we consider has the highest probability, a probability formed by hundreds and thousands of previous experiences seeing the same thing (rectangular shapes). We live in a world of right angles and we expect right angles. He demonstrated that we were prepared to see a red ball float through the air instead of question our perception. I was listening and examining my own perceptions.

At the end of the experiment the speaker related this to education, training, and leadership. He said someday managers and educators would work to develop their employees' and students' perception. They would assign tasks that methodically developed a perception of competency, a real sense that "I can do this, and more."

He said that the way to build this perception of capability was to give a series of assignments that increase in difficulty and, at the same time, provide adequate support such that the person succeeds in accomplishing each task along the way. This would build the individual's perception that they could solve problems and handle even bigger and bigger ones. This was in contrast to the prevailing idea of throwing someone into a situation and seeing if they would "sink or swim." He gave the example of the space program where the astronauts, after years of training, had the perception that they could do it, their ground crew could do it, and their equipment could do it—get to the moon and back safely.

As I listened to this I realized that the "someday" when this was common practice was too far in the future for me. I recognized the unintended consequence of years of cancelled projects was my perception that my future IBM projects would be cancelled. But now I wanted to change that perception. I wanted the projects that I worked on to be successful. This class gave me the formula for building perception: start with simple projects and build to more complex projects and ensure success along the way. I began to formulate a plan for myself. I needed a project that I could do, and complete, in a short period of time. Recognizing that FS was not the right project for my goal, I kept my eyes open for something else.

My opportunity came along not too long after I returned from this class. IBM had recently announced the IBM 3800[45], a high-speed continuous forms laser printer. Imagine printing stacks of fan-fold pages of bank statements or medical bills. The paper literally flew through the printer. The printer was supported on the latest IBM/370 MVS[46] operating system under the spooling[47] system JES2 (Job Entry Subsystem[48]). But, there were important IBM customers who still had the older IBM computers running the MVT[49] operating system and using HASP (Houston Automatic Spooling Priority[50]). The scientific community, in particular, wanted access to this new, high-speed, laser printer but they did not want to upgrade to the latest operating system. There was enough demand from this community that IBM responded. The project was to retrofit the new IBM 3800 printer into the HASP spooling system.

I knew nothing about spooling systems or printers. I had worked as an applications programmer and this project would lead me into the realm of systems programming. But I was assured that it was easy. I was a programmer, after all. It was a two-person project and should take less than a year to implement. I worked with Thom Scrutchin, whose mind flew from one idea to the next in intuitive leaps. My logical approach struggled to keep up with him. Thom knew the history of HASP. Originally designed and written by IBM for the Johnson Space Center in Houston, it handled the relatively slower process of reading punched cards or printing data, thereby allowing the CPU to run programs quickly and "spool" their output files for later printing. He told me stories of Tom Simpson, the developer of HASP, who would go to the HASP user meetings, listen to their requests, control the direction of the discussions to some extent and then at the end of the meeting announce that these new functions were already implemented and in the next version of HASP.

We acquired the HASP source code and I began work. Slowly the concepts of spooling and job printing became second nature to me. Soon I was writing the detailed instructions to read the print files, determine what fonts were needed by the file, download the fonts followed by the data in order to drive the 3800 printer. I retrofitted these instructions into the framework of the existing HASP code.

The 3800 printer emulated a line printer[51] and printed lines of text using up to four downloadable fonts. I made some innovations. My objective was to keep the printer running as fast as possible, but while the fonts were downloading, the printer was not printing. When my routine started the next print file, it checked to see if it was using the same four fonts as the previous job, and if so, it skipped the step of downloading the fonts and immediately started transmitting the data. This kept the printer running. Previously the code just automatically downloaded the fonts without checking to see if they had changed. My optimization minimized the time between jobs.

Traditionally, printing speed was measured by how long it took to print a job and a thousand page print job could keep the 3800 printing at rated speed. With my optimization, shorter jobs that used the same fonts also printed at rated speed. Thom recommended that I call the JES2 development team and describe how I was optimizing font downloading. The idea seemed so simple to me that I was reluctant to think it was anything innovative. Thom insisted and I called. But the phone call was not satisfactory because whoever I spoke with responded with a "so what" attitude. I have often felt that he just mirrored my "it's nothing much" opinion.

Now it was time for testing. We needed a computer with the 3800 printer and somehow Thom arranged it. IBM was constructing a new building, especially designed for its programming staff, in south San Jose called the Santa Teresa Laboratory. The building was finished and the computer facility was up and running but no employees were working there yet. We managed to get access to the computing facility and their IBM 3800 printer for my testing. Since no one else was working there the computer response time was excellent. Also, I could get into the main computer room to work directly with the 3800 printer. Soon I was no longer working in Palo Alto but working at the Santa Teresa Lab, another 45-minute commute.

As the testing proceeded we now needed to update the manuals in order to ship this new version of HASP. At this time an internal writing department created all IBM publications and product documentation. When we approached them for our documentation needs we discovered that they could not fit our project into their schedule in a timely manner. This could easily have been a roadblock for the project. But we contracted to have this work done outside of IBM. This way the manuals were written and ready when the product was ready. We completed the work and the manuals and shipped the project in under a year.

I had done it! A completed, successful project!

In February 1977, while working on this project, I found myself crying uncontrollable on a late Sunday evening.

Unbeknownst to me, my father, now retired and living with his second wife in Seattle, suddenly collapsed and died. He was always supportive of my career and proud of my accomplishments, but he never learned about this latest one.

1978-1979
Detour into Management

As I was finishing the 3800 project I received an offer for a position as a manager in the IBM San Jose Research Lab. The staff there remembered me from my summer internship and recommended me for the position. As I was about to accept this offer, I received some advice from a colleague. He told me that the Research Division was known for not promoting programmers and engineers since most of the employees were Research Staff Members and the positions of programmers and engineers were in support roles. He recommended that I get promoted before I accept the job. This was good advice and I followed it.

My last promotion was in 1972 when I became a Staff Programmer. The next level was Advisory Programmer. I took a look at the job description for Advisory Programmer. It was a long, detailed list of performance activities and duties. As I read the description I recognized that I was already performing at that level. My manager probably did not realize everything I had done on the 3800 project since he had left all the details of design and implementation to Thom and me. I needed to convince my manager to take the time to write-up and submit the documentation for my promotion.

But he was busy with other things and he did not have the necessary information.

So I prepared the documentation for him. I wrote detailed descriptions of the actions I had taken on the project demonstrating that I met each requirement for Advisory Programmer. Only when this was complete did I approach my manager. All he had to do was agree with my documentation and sign the paperwork authorizing the promotion. It was a different way of relating with a manager because I basically did all his work. But even in this I was displaying that I operated at the advisory level. The promotion came through immediately.

San Jose Research was looking for a manager of the User Interface Department in the newly established Research Computing Facility. During the 1970s there was one computing center for all of IBM in San Jose at Cottle Road. This was a time of centralized computing using large mainframe computers and requiring a technical staff to keep everything running. But the diverse community of computer users in the various divisions of IBM in San Jose had different requirements, from running the purchasing programs to running scientific experiments. Whenever there was a question of which group had the priority for the computer time, research always fell behind the demands of production.

Dr. Henry Gladney had presented a successful argument to IBM higher management to split off an independent computing facility for IBM Research's exclusive use, and now he was staffing this new department. Within the Research Computing Facility he wanted a department that would interface between the Research Staff Members (chemists, physicists, and computer scientists) and the new computing center. He called it a User Interface Department and it would be responsible for user documentation and education, for a user forum, and for determining and installing software to satisfy users' requests. It would be a department with four or five employees to assist in the responsibilities. He told me that the Research Staff Members, especially some of the physicists who had long, complicated computer programs, were unhappy with the previous computer center decisions. They could be very vocal and demanding. Did I want the job?

I had not been looking to go into management. I liked technical work: solving the problems. But it looked like a new challenge and I said, "Yes."

After I had accepted the position, he told me that he was interviewing John Thomas for the position to install and support the operating systems. I remembered John from when I first started work at IBM and I knew that he was extremely knowledgeable about operating systems. Dr. Henry Gladney asked my opinion, "Do you think I should try to hire John Thomas for operating system support?"

"No," I responded. Henry looked startled when I said that so emphatically until I continued with: "I don't think you should *try* to hire him. I think you *should* hire him."

There was one more department of computer operators that kept the machines running 24 hours a day by scheduling jobs then mounting magnetic tapes or disk drives if the job required a special device. In addition these operators ran the daily, weekly, and monthly backups of the computer data and sent copies to Iron Mountain[52] for storage.

As I started in this new management position, I received some advice from a family friend, Earl Scott. Earl was one of the original founders of Tektronix Corporation, and had some excellent management experience. He said, "You only have to be right just over 50% of the time on your decisions. Remember, Babe Ruth, who had the most home runs, also had the most strikeouts at bat."

He must have known something about me that I was just beginning to recognize for myself: that I do not want to make mistakes. It probably made me a good programmer, but being cautious was not an admirable attribute for a manager. I could not imagine being wrong 10% of the time, much less 48% of the time. I never was able to practically integrate his advice and agonized over my management decisions.

This management position was a very difficult time for me. Something shifted in me when I had the manager title, as if I had taken on a new way of being with this new role. I could feel my change in attitude, a different posture even, but I seemed to have no control over it. I was told, "Hey, we liked what you did and how you worked. That's why we recommended you for the position. You don't have to change." But somehow the title "manager" never sat comfortably on my shoulders.

When I took the job as manager of the User Interface Department, I was assigned a group of employees that had been in the San Jose Research Lab for years and moved into my department. I didn't have any say in the hiring except when, about a year later, I brought in another employee. The employees I inherited each brought their own challenges, especially in terms of upsets with their previous managers.

I recognized that my wanting to please everyone did not bode well for being a manager. I listened to my employees and wanted to supply the things they needed to do their job. But when I met with my manager and I listened to his requests I soon realized that I was getting squished in-between these two groups. I was not strong enough, in my own self, to stand up forcefully to these two conflicting demands.

In addition we had a challenging group of computer users. Our department was running the user forum, we were installing software, and we were publishing a computer users' newsletter. But I felt that I was swimming in deep water. Then the physicists approached my manager and challenged my competence for the job. This was my worse case scenario: everyone was upset with me. Henry stood up for me, but when he told me what they said to him, it undermined my already shaky self-confidence. I felt pretty defeated. Their critical comments magnified my internal self-criticism. This was perhaps the low point in my career.

One employee challenged me in a provocative way. He posted a nude photograph of his girlfriend on his wall. I requested that he take it down. He said that he would if I put the request in writing. Well, I did put it in writing and he did take it down. But years later he mailed me that copy of the letter. I guess it was supposed to embarrass me in some way. I never understood his motivation.

One employee was obviously not performing, according to the other managers. I apparently did not see the issue the same way, or I was reluctant to confront the problem. Most likely I was reluctant, so I did not see it. Once, when I was away on a business trip, another manager sat in for me during my absence and took drastic steps and got the employee into an alcohol recovery program.

I am not proud of my time as a manager, but I did learn some things from it. In one case, one of my employees had explored all the possible versions of the Fortran Compiler. He had spoken with the chemists and physicists to see what would be the most suitable compiler for their work. Then he came to me and asked me to make a decision about which one to install. I remember listening to his presentation and realizing that I did not have the depth of experience on this issue that he did. It seemed to me that he should be making the recommendation for which one to install. He was reluctant to make the call, but eventually I convinced him that he was the most knowledgeable person to select the compiler; after all, he had just studied the issues. Later in my career I remembered this occasion. Being a manager taught me to be a much better employee and to take more responsibility when making recommendations to management. Later in my career I had the reputation of managing my manager.

I remember one success during this time. We were converting the computing center to a new computer with a new operating system. We scheduled a meeting to inform the researcher staff of the changes and the actions they needed to take so their existing programs would run on the new system. I was leading this meeting. My usual internal dialogue, that constantly questioned my ability, was quiet this time. I focused on all the information that was needed for this migration. The day unfolded like magic for me. As I was preparing for the next set of slides for my presentation, the person who had the information I needed walked into my office.

"What do the users need to know about the conversion of their data?" I asked.

He had the answers and we agreed that I would introduce him to discuss that topic. Then I wanted to have a dry run of my presentation before the scheduled meeting. The next person to enter my office was one of the other computer center managers, the one who questioned me the most.

"I want to know what you are going to say," he barked.

"Good," I said, "I wanted to have an opportunity to run-through my presentation." When I finished, he left my office feeling much better, assured that all the necessary subjects were being covered.

At the meeting, with all the challenging scientists present, I walked everyone through the steps for the conversion from one computing system to the next. At the end, I received a comment from one of the most technical guys on the computing center staff when John Thomas said, "I didn't realize we were in such good shape." Coming from him, that was a high compliment.

The Research Division was small enough that as a manager in the computing center I started to see the interdependencies of all the departments. If I wanted something from the personnel department (like hiring a new employee) or from the facilities department (for office space and equipment), they, in turn, came to my department for their computer support. One organizational observation I made concerned the copy department. This was a time when the copy machines were large and expensive. A separate department, with a manager and employees, made all the copies. Lunchtime conversations often devolved into complaints about the copy department with comments on the delays and inefficiencies. When I dealt with the copy department, I had no problems. But its reputation continued and I realized that every new employee, after listening to the lunchtime complaints, was predisposed to approach the copy department and expect problems. This allowed me to see how a corporate culture gets carried on for years.

At noon, I would go running with some of the other research employees. We left the IBM site and drove to the other side of the freeway to run along the path next to Coyote Creek. This group was training together because two women from the IBM San Jose Research Lab were on the Annapurna[53] climb, an all-women's climb of the tenth highest peak in the world. I heard discussions about planning meetings, about who was going to the base camp, about how much rice to carry in, how many Sherpas were needed to carry all that rice, how much more rice was needed to feed those additional Sherpas. All this information was swirling around me, but I was not involved except that I joined the group to run at noon, when I could.

Two women made it to the top of Annapurna. One was Irene Beardsley from the IBM San Jose Research Lab. Two women were killed in a fall. One was Vera Watson from IBM San Jose Research Lab. When I heard the preliminary report that there had been an accident, I did not want to believe it. I would not believe it until it was confirmed. Yet it was true. Vera Watson, who I had been jogging with at noon only months earlier had fallen on the summit attempt and was lost. I remember my devastation the morning I read the confirming article in the newspaper. That climb is well documented in the book *Annapurna: A Woman's Place* by Arlene Blum[54].

1980
Personal Changes

The 1970s had been a challenging decade for me. Now, at the beginning of the '80s, things started to turn a corner. In April of 1980 I went on a blind date and met a man who became my dear and wonderful husband. Mutual friends suggested that we meet when this man said he was interested in meeting a tall, independent woman with a sense of adventure. Ed Downing, himself well over six feet tall, never thought that my 5'8" qualified as tall, but he did like my independence and sense of adventure. He was living on a sailboat in Santa Cruz harbor and worked as a computer programmer for the medical industry in Santa Clara.

Our first adventure together was to sail from Santa Cruz harbor to Stillwater Cove near Pebble Beach over the Fourth of July weekend. On the return sail, as the seas built, I was on the foredeck fumbling with the intricacies of tying a bowline knot on the jib sheet. I was nervous in these conditions and tied it wrong several times. He waited patiently, steering into the waves to give me a more level platform, saying, "Take your time." He never once complained that I was taking too long. He had a love of sailing and was very comfortable in all situations. This instilled my confidence in him.

Early in our relationship we both started using our full names. For me it was a matter of claiming the beautiful name that had been given to me, Katherine. He also had a handsome name, Edmund. By September I had met his children when we all went on a backpacking trip together: Todd, then twelve, with the teenager in him just around the corner, who did not think adults could be trusted if they did not fill the canteens with water before setting off on a hike; Sara, at seven, who would say she was tired but then run ahead when she saw a bird rustling in the bushes; and Gavin, almost four, who carried his own backpack and was a real trouper.

By October, Edmund and I were living together in my small house in Palo Alto. The children came over to visit every other weekend, or we would go camping on what we called "friends weekends," or trips to the Sierra for ski weekends. Two years later we married in Sausalito, California, on a full moon and a high tide. It was New Year's Eve and we sailed away from the reception on Edmund's trimaran sailboat, *The Redwood Coast*.

We rarely talked about our computer jobs; they became a backdrop for our adventures together. Edmund soon left his programming job in the medical industry and started his own computer consulting firm: Downing Associates, Inc. In the beginning he worked at a client's site and had several long-term programming projects. Later he worked from home as he developed the programs to his client's specifications. This worked out especially well when his three children came to live with us full time in the summer of 1984.

But I am getting ahead of myself.

1980
Text Processing Tools

In the spring of 1980 I was walking down the hall outside my office at the IBM San Jose Research Lab when I saw Jim King coming toward me. Jim King was in the Research Computer Science Department, the same department where I had been a summer intern years earlier. He was one of the PhDs who researched new ideas for computers, and he had a reputation for being outspoken. I remembered seeing a recent announcement that Jim had received a Research Division Award and I stopped to congratulate him.

"Jim, congratulations on the award you just received." I had not read the announcement very carefully so I asked, "What did you get it for?"

He looked at me and snapped, "For doing your job!"

I was stunned and walked away without further comment.

This incident upset me very much. I was hurt by the sharpness of it. I was bewildered, thinking, what could he possibly mean, "my job?" As the day wore on I could not get over my upset. Working as manager of the User Interface Department of the Research Computing Facility, my department played a support role to the scientists. We had the responsibility to install software on the computers for the scientists to use.

That evening I thought more about this encounter in the hall, still troubled by Jim's comment. I was taking a workshop, outside of IBM, that had a very definite ground rule: "If you have an upset you must clear it up immediately or not be in the workshop." How was I going to clear it up? I needed to talk to Jim King and clarify his comment so I decided that I would invite him for coffee the next day and have this discussion. I thought about several ways I could begin the conversation.

The next day I called Jim King and he agreed to meet me that morning in the cafeteria.

As we sat down I said, "Jim, you said something yesterday that…"

"I know," he jumped in before I had finished, "It was very unfair of me to say that."

He defused my upset immediately by his apology and the recognition of the unfairness of his comment. I then learned why he had received the award.

Jim had installed a text processing program on one of the main computers that greatly helped the computer science staff. It was, indeed, the responsibility of my department to install software for use by the scientists, and there was a demand for new text processing tools. But my manager had explicitly forbidden me to work in this area. He did not want me to install new text processing tools because he was using the demand to justify to his own management that he needed more staff (called head-count) assigned to the department to take on this additional task. So Jim found the software and installed it, totally bypassing the politics of the Computing Facility staff. And this is why Jim said he was doing my job. His immediate apology allowed me to see beyond Jim's gruff exterior. He did not become less gruff or more diplomatic, but never again did anything he said offend me.

In that spring of 1980, when I met Edmund, my manager continued to restrict me from working on installing new text processing tools. But the demand for new tools was not going away. Then, within a short period of time, there was a management change when Jim McCrossin arrived from back east to become the new manager of the Research Computing Facility. I remember my first interview with him.

"What do you see as the priorities for your department?" he asked.

"I think we need to install modern text processing tools," I responded.

"How would you go about that?" he asked.

"I would have a task force to review what is available. Once we understood the options we would make a recommendation," I replied.

"Do it," he said, and that ended the conversation.

Now I had the responsibility and the authorization to work on this problem.

The scientists at the IBM San Jose Research Lab were always writing papers and submitting them to journals. As you can imagine, you cannot write anything scientific without using special characters: even water (H two O) requires a subscript 2: H_2O. At that time the members of the Manuscript Processing Center typed these papers and printed them on an IBM Selectric typewriter[55]. Whenever a special character was needed the typists would include a special stop code in the document. When the document was printed, the Selectric typewriter stopped when it encountered the special code. The women in the Manuscript Processing Center removed the standard type ball and inserted the special character type ball. These women, after they had typed the document for the scientists, would sit and babysit the Selectric typewriter and change the type ball hundreds of times while the document printed.

When the document went off to a scientific journal it had to be "camera ready"—ready to be photocopied into the journal. Any images, diagrams, or graphics were created independent of the text and merged onto the "camera ready" pages.

In the task force we found out about some software written at the IBM Yorktown Research Lab called the Yorktown Mathematical Formula Processor (YMFP). It allowed the typist to type an equation the same way it would be read aloud, for instance: "(x squared plus y squared) over 2." The program chose the special characters, chose the size of the characters, the fonts and the size of the subscripts and superscripts. These documents could not be printed on the Selectric typewriter or on the printer in the computer room. It required a different type of printer, not a line printer, but a dot matrix printer so that the symbols could be placed in any position above and below the text line. Since most documents were revised multiple times before they were "camera ready" and because the "camera ready" printer was an expensive phototypesetter, we needed a proof printer for all the intermediate copies. The phototypesetter paper and supplies cost over a dollar per page, so the proof printer had to be pennies per page.

I went to the IBM Yorktown Research Lab in New York to see their installation with the formula processor and the proof printer—a dot matrix Versatec[56] printer. I met the people who had installed their system. I returned to San Jose and reported to my manager.

I outlined the tasks required to install the Yorktown Mathematical Formula Processor and the Versatec printer for the proof copies. The expensive, phototypesetter printer, shared by all the local IBM divisions, was located in one of the nearby buildings. I would need to augment the fonts available on the phototypesetter to include the fonts with the special characters needed by the Research Staff. The software ran on the VM/CMS[57] operating system that was already installed and running in the Research Computing Facility. We needed to write a new set of CMS EXECs[58] to provide the users easy access to the formula processor, proof printer, and phototypesetter.

Jim McCrossin listened to my outline and responded. "I'll create a new department to handle these responsibilities. You can be the manager and have two or three staff. It will be the Text Processing Department. What do you think?"

As I sat there and listened I thought about the problems involved in coordinating a staff to install the software and printers. I thought about my department employees who were on the task force with me but who contributed very little. "I would rather do the technical work myself and not have a department to manage," I replied.

Jim took my statement at face value and acted quickly. The next day I was no longer a manager. I reported to Jim

McCrossin directly. I was responsible for installing this software and educating the users.

This challenging technical project was very enjoyable and rewarding on many levels.

From my previous experience as a manager, I knew how to work with my new manager. Instead of bringing him problems, I brought him solutions. Every other week I met with him to provide a status update. Whenever I prepared for these meetings I would outline the current problems I was facing. Then I would indicate what I proposed to do to solve each situation. Jim sat and listened.

One problem I needed to solve was to find or build a cable to connect the Versatec printer to the VM/CMS computer. This was a hardware problem. I was a software programmer. But unlike in my previous job, I did not spend any time thinking that I could not solve it. I did not have any internal conversation that this would be difficult, nor that I did not know enough to solve this problem, nor that I would never get it done on time, nor any of the other internal conversations that just wastes time. Instead, I kept talking to the people in Yorktown and following leads.

Someone suggested that I check for a suitable cable in one of the labs upstairs. I walked into the lab and met Sig Nin. I explained what I was looking for and he knew the solution. Over the next few years I worked on projects with Sig and I found him to be an exceptionally capable person, one who was always helpful.

With the cable problem solved I had the Versatec printer installed and working. I installed the Yorktown Mathematical Formula Processor software, wrote the CMS EXECs, and printed sample output on the Versatec printer.

The next step was to print the "camera ready" output on the phototypesetter printer. I met with my manager and outlined the problem and my plan for the solution.

"The phototypesetter is a very expensive piece of equipment and we cannot afford to purchase our own. All the departments that use the phototypesetter are meeting soon to select the set of fonts to be purchased for the typesetter. Because Research documents need fonts with all the special characters, I'll attend these meeting and represent our interests. Who knows how long this will take?"

Before the meetings occurred—just getting everyone notified and in the same room took some time—I went to check out the phototypesetter printer. There I met the lead technician who operated the printer. I told him I was from Research and we needed some fonts with special characters.

"No problem," he said. "When the Research jobs come in, I'll just load this other font disk with the fonts you want." He picked up what looked like a cover for a cake; it was about twelve inches in diameter, four inches high, and heavier than a cake cover. It was a disk pack that contained the fonts we needed.

That was it, the solution for printing the final "camera ready" copies. I did not have to attend any of the meetings to negotiate fonts. Research had a separate disk pack with its own set of fonts. I reported the status to Jim and he gave me the greatest compliment when he said, "You manage much better when you don't have the title." Instead of working competitively within the hierarchy of divisions and management levels, I could forge a path with cooperation.

With the software and hardware in place, I began to educate the users. I started with the Manuscript Processing Center. There were about five young women who worked in this center. The scientists dropped off hand-written documents, the young women in the Manuscript Processing Center typed the documents and returned a proof copy to the scientists. After several rounds of rewrites and corrections the document was ready to be sent to the phototypesetter for the final copy. These young women were bright and capable and they learned the new system very quickly. They were happy to be rid of the tedious process of printing documents on the Selectric typewriter.

Then I offered training and classes to the scientific staff on this new process for creating documents. Soon the scientists saw how easy it was to use the Yorktown Mathematical Formula Processor and they started to type their own documents into the computer and print out their proof and final copies. This gave them greater independence, since they were no longer dependent on the workload in the Manuscript Processing Center.

I enjoyed doing the technical work and providing the training to the staff. I noticed that I had a very positive way of working with whomever I was training. Since the training was often one-on-one, I was able to recognize the level of understanding of the individual and present the material accordingly. I never made someone feel inadequate for not understanding and that made it easier for them to learn and be successful. I recognized this in retrospect since it was not something I was conscious of doing at the time.

Designing and writing programs was easy in the 1980s using the VM/CMS environment where the display terminal in my office connected to the mainframe computer. There was an internal network, like an Internet, connecting all the VM/CMS computer systems at the various IBM locations. Unlike the Internet, the internal network did not have websites but did provide a method for exchanging files of data and messages between all the employees. Each morning when I arrived at work and logged onto the computer terminal in my office I could query and find out who else was online across the company. I used this facility frequently to communicate to other colleagues, especially when I was installing the formula processor and had a question for someone in Yorktown. Often I would formulate my question but before sending the message, I would have figured out the answer to my problem and just deleted the message without sending it. On other occasions, if I had sent the message and no longer needed their response, or if I had inadvertently transmitted it before it was complete, I could recall the message. It was useful to have this option.

I was still working in the triangular San Jose Research building on Cottle Road when one day, while I was having lunch with colleagues on the outside cafeteria patio, the earth began to shake. "Earthquake!" we all said in unison. We watched as all the cars in the nearby parking lot rocked back and forth on their suspension, looking like boats rocking in a harbor. Our building did not sustain any damage but there were concerns for our future safety. With the recent changes in building codes, a decision was made to reinforce the building from the outside—to build something like a buttress for lateral support. Then it was decided to build a building around the current building. Soon I was working in the middle of a construction site.

Before construction began, the external stairwells, one of which was located near my office, were destroyed. A crane with a wrecking ball pounded the concrete stairwells to dust. This constant hammering made it very difficult to concentrate. Some of the research staff had moved to temporary trailers that were set up in the parking lots. I was still working for the Research Computing Facility on text processing tools but most of the work was complete, and I was getting bored as I sat in my office on the second floor overlooking the glass-enclosed computer room.

Fortunately, a new assignment came my way. Jim King, who worked in the Research Computer Science Department, approached my manager to ask if I could come and work, on loan, in his department on a project that he was starting. When Jim explained the project to me I was very pleased to accept this new opportunity: both for the work assignment (writing software to drive an experimental printer) and the new location (working in the temporary trailers away from the construction zone). The acronym for this project was SHERPA: San jHose Experimental Rasterizing Printer Attachment.

1981-1983
SHERPA Experimental Printer

The SHERPA control unit was designed by Jim King and Ben Milander to provide an alternate data path to the IBM 6670 laser printer. This printer, announced by IBM in late 1979, functioned like a high-speed mainframe line printer, but it was physically smaller in size (about 6'x3'x3.5'), and it was attached to the mainframe computer over telephone communication lines instead of the big black cable running under the computer room floor. This allowed the printer to be placed outside the computer center for use as a local departmental printer. So instead of walking to the computer center to pick up your printed output, you could pick it up from a printer located near your office: a departmental printer.

The microcode (hardware-level instructions) in the 6670 provided a traditional line printer interface to the user. The user could print lines of text using characters from one of four fonts. The fact that the 6670 emulated a line printer provided compatibility to all the pre-existing programs so they could print on this printer without modification. But beneath this line printer interface the 6670 internal microcode created a raster graphic image[59] or bitmap[60] of the complete page before transferring this bitmap to the laser print mechanism. This bitmap specified where to place the ink on the paper; it was a two-dimensional data array with one bit for each point on the page. The 6670 had 300 pixels[61] per inch.

"There's a lot of function in the 6670 that's not exposed at the user level," Jim King recognized. "We need to drive that print head ourselves. If we could only get access at the level of the laser print mechanism of the 6670, bypassing their microcode that makes it look like a line printer, we could build our own bitmap that includes text, images, and graphics on the same page."

Jim King negotiated with the IBM 6670 developers in Boulder, Colorado, and obtained a hardware interface to the 6670 print mechanism. Then Jim along with Ben Milander, previously from the ASDD model shop, designed and built a special-purpose hardware control unit: the SHERPA control unit. Its function was to connect to the mainframe computer over a communications line, process a set of commands to build a bitmap image of the page, and deliver that bitmap to the 6670 print mechanism. The SHERPA control unit microcode implemented a set of commands that provided the users the ability to place not only text but also images and graphics into the bitmap. The SHERPA control unit made the 6670 all-points-addressable[62] (capable of referencing any pixel on the page) instead of line addressable.

Sig Nin worked on the SHERPA project and wrote the microcode inside the SHERPA control unit. I wrote the host VM/370 software that took a printer file and converted it into the commands to drive the SHERPA microcode. The file could be a simple computer listing or the output of text processing applications. The most common text processing file type produced by IBM text processing applications was

AFPDS[63], an acronym for Advanced Function Printer Data Stream.

The AFPDS files used a set of fonts specifically designed for IBM printers. The fonts, Sonoran San Serif or Sonoran Serif, were purchased from font designers who were artists and vocal about the size and shape of the individual characters in a font. Each font character, represented as a bitmap, came in a variety of sizes: 10-point, 11-point, 12-point, etc., and two resolutions: 300 pels (dots or picture elements) per inch or 600 pels per inch. The font designers were adamant that a 10-point font could not be scaled to a larger size. Instead each font character must be designed for each size and resolution. The characters were not fixed width but variable width. A width table was provided for each font that specified the width, in pels, for each character. I was very familiar with the Sonoran fonts and their corresponding width tables.

The VM host software I wrote processed the AFPDS file and downloaded the bitmap for a font character into the SHERPA memory the first time the character occurred in the document, and then I referenced the already-downloaded character for subsequent uses. I specified a coordinate location (x, y) on the bitmap in the SHERPA page, followed by a microcode command that moved the stored character to that location. Whereas on the IBM 3800 project I downloaded an entire font, even if only one or two characters were used, for the SHERPA I only downloaded the bitmap for the specific characters used by the document. Again I kept track of what fonts and characters were already loaded in the SHERPA memory as my program transmitted the lines of data to be printed on the page.

In addition to processing text documents, I wrote software routines to convert image files into SHERPA microcode commands to print images on the page. An image was a very large bitmap that was not saved in the SHERPA memory, where a character bitmap was saved, but went directly into the page bitmap at a specific location.

For graphics, I defined a file format with a simple set of graphic commands that corresponded to the commands defined by Jim King for the SHERPA microcode. This format was simple enough for the users to convert their existing graphic file format into this set of graphic commands. My software routines read these graphics files and converted them into the microcode commands to draw lines and arcs on the SHERPA modified 6670, the SHERPA printer.

Thus, we offered the user the ability to print a page composed with text, image, and graphics. This seems common today, but at that time it was a new idea to combine these functions in one printer.

Since the font designers were so adamant about the integrity of the character bitmaps, we did not look at expressing the characters as a mathematical equation that could be scaled for each font size. But this was the breakthrough that was needed to get away from the cumbersome bitmap font files. This was the breakthrough that Adobe Systems[64] made in their representation of fonts in PostScript[65] files. Adobe Systems was founded in 1982 by former Xerox PARC[66] employees. PostScript was licensed to Apple Inc.[67] in 1985 sparking the desktop publishing[68] revolution.

The SHERPA was an experimental printer in 1981. There were only a handful of us working on it. Jim King was the overall project leader. With only a few people it was easy to make design changes and improvements and to debug problems. So often on projects when something goes wrong everyone starts blaming the other guy. The more people who work on a project the more options there are to find someone else to blame. Even if it is not overt blame, the cause of the problem is often difficult to sort out. But with only two of us working on the data transfer (my software was creating the data commands that Sig Nin's microcode was processing), we usually could quickly discover the problem when the output page looked nothing like what we expected. We did have some very unusual printed pages at the beginning.

Jim King made lots of recommendations for new function in the host software I was writing. Since he designed the interfaces between the SHERPA unit, the 6670 printer and the mainframe VM/370 system, he knew what additional function was available.

For instance, the SHERPA unit communicated the status of the printer back to the mainframe computer and my host software. Since the 6670 was a remote departmental printer, someone near the printer, not the computer center staff, needed to know the status of the printer. I implemented the concept of a printer owner and delivered a message to that person's terminal whenever the printer was out of paper or had a paper jam. Then I sent a message to the document owner when their document finished printing, giving them immediate feedback that it was ready to be picked up. We never had this type of notification from the printers attached to the mainframe computers in the computer room.

Once we had everything working on our first SHERPA printer we installed it for general use in the IBM San Jose Research Lab. It was very well received and soon all the 6670 printers in the building were running with the SHERPA control units. Pat Mantey, an upper-level manager in the Research Computer Science Department, arranged to have SHERPA units installed in IBM Science Centers and at various universities across the country. The goal was to get feedback about the function and usability of the new interface to the printer. Jim King hired a technician, Barney, to build more SHERPA control units.

When I heard about the plan to install SHERPAs at all these various locations, I became interested in coordinating the installations. I requested that responsibility and it was gratefully extended to me. I contacted each location to determine the name of the person I would be working with. I reviewed with them all the prerequisites for the project: an IBM 6670 printer and a communications line to a VM/370 system. Once this was in place I traveled to each location with a copy of my software and a SHERPA Control Unit. Usually in less than half a day the system would be up and working at their location. Most locations were labs where they had a requirement for printing graphics. I went to Stanford University and installed one at the Stanford Linear Accelerator Lab. Before I left that afternoon, they had written a program to convert their graphic files to the graphic interface I had defined for the SHERPA, and were printing their graphics files.

I installed one at the University of California in Berkeley, one at the Naval Research Post Graduate School in Monterey, and one at Princeton University. As I visited these locations I noticed how familiar their computing environment was to me. The people I met spoke a similar language. I provided them with an easily accessible new printing capability. They were pleased. I was satisfied.

IBM had a number of Science Centers around the country. One was in Palo Alto, California, three were in Europe: Heidelberg, Rome, and Paris. I installed a SHERPA system in all these Science Centers. At the Palo Alto Science Center, I met Robert Creasy. He was one of the original team that created the IBM Virtual Machine/Virtual Memory operating system CP-40[69] which went on to become the VM/370 and the CMS operating system.

Installing the SHERPAs at the Heidelberg Science Center, Rome Science Center, and Paris Science Center offered some unique experiences for me. It was the fall of 1983. Edmund and I had been married about eight months. In 1968 Edmund had lived in Heidelberg, when he was in the Army, so we decided to take a European vacation to correspond with the installations and to travel for two weeks before I started to work. We would fly to Frankfurt, drive to Heidelberg, through southern Germany, then take the train to Venice and Rome. A month before we started our trip, I had completed the international documentation and shipped the SHERPA control units to each location. The SHERPA hardware technician, Barney, was to meet me in Heidelberg to deal with any hardware issues.

When Edmund and I arrived in Heidelberg for our vacation days, I could not resist the opportunity to find the Heidelberg Science Center and introduce myself. I learned that they did not have their SHERPA control unit yet. It was somewhere in customs, but they felt it would surely be there in two weeks when I returned for the installation. When we traveled to Rome I decided to check on the status of things at the Rome Science Center. It was located outside of Rome and Edmund and I took a cab out to their lab one day. They also did not have their control unit yet as it was also held up in customs. I decided to install my VM software for them on their mainframe while I was there. It was a pleasure for me to sit at the terminal in a small office in the IBM Rome Science Center and train the local staff. I was teaching them how to install and configure my software programs for their specific needs. Edmund was sitting across the room while I worked. It was the first time he was present while I was performing my IBM professional duties, and he got to see a side of me that he did not normally see.

After our two-week vacation, Edmund flew back to California and I returned to Heidelberg. When I arrived Monday morning with Barney at the Heidelberg Science Center we learned that the SHERPA control unit was still hung up in customs. By the end of the day we learned that it was in Frankfurt, but it would not be delivered for several days. I had allocated two to three days for each installation, and a delay of several days would ruin our schedule. One of the staff members suggested hiring a car and driver to retrieve the SHERPA from customs. This was a good idea. They would leave immediately and the unit would be on site the next morning. The next morning arrived but the driver had not picked up the SHERPA. "It wouldn't fit in the car," he said. Only about the size of a large breadbox, it had been packed in a box as big as a small table. The driver did not know that he could have unpacked it.

Now it was Tuesday and we were leaving for Rome on Wednesday. Barney and I had a rental car during our stay in Heidelberg and we decided to drive to Frankfurt and pick up the unit ourselves. The Heidelberg staff looked at me and I felt they were thinking, "This American, she thinks things can happen when she wants them to happen." Barney and I drove on the autobahn for about an hour until we reached Frankfurt. We located the customs warehouse and found the box containing the SHERPA unit. We unpacked the box, put the control unit on the back seat of the car and drove the hour back to the Heidelberg Science Center. By the end of the day everything was installed and working.

Barney was traveling with a satchel full of instruments and tools that he had brought to solve any hardware problem that might come up. Before we left the Heidelberg Science Center for our flight to Rome, the staff asked us if we wanted the special paperwork for transporting the tools into Italy. This was a new concept for us. Couldn't we just travel with our tools? Finally we convinced them that we did not need any special papers for our carry-on bag. The hardware we were importing, the SHERPA control unit, already had all its customs paperwork completed. A few hours later we landed in Rome and we were stopped for an inspection. The clerk pointed to Barney's satchel and questioned, in Italian, what was in it. We attempted several English responses to his inquiry but when we said, "It is for repairs," we were immediately released to enter Italy. We figured that everything in Italy must need repair so they let us in with our tools.

When we arrived back at the Rome Science Center they still had not received their SHERPA control unit. I told them how we found the one in Frankfurt customs. They made some more inquires but still it could not be located or delivered in a timely manner. I had already installed the software and trained the staff in Rome so Barney and I decided to continue on to Paris where we would install their system since they had received their SHERPA control unit. Then he would return to Rome early the next week after they received their unit.

Paris was a wonderful whirlwind. I stayed in the most beautiful hotel on a narrow side street. The decorations and color combinations were so elegant that I wanted to stay forever. The installation at the Paris Science Center went without any problems in less than half a day. The staff could not understand why I was leaving so soon to return to California. I, too, was tempted to stay and enjoy Paris, but a friend was getting married on the weekend and I wanted to be at her wedding.

I returned to San Jose to wrap up the loose ends on the SHEPRA project and look for what was next. I was on loan from the Research Computing Facility while I worked on the SHERPA project in the Research Computer Science Department. When I started looking around for another assignment, Don Chamberlain, my on-loan manager, said that he did not want to hire me away from the computing facility, but if I were looking for a new position, he would like to hire me for the Computer Science Department. Remembering what the atmosphere was like a few years earlier when I did a summer internship, I said I did not expect to stay in the Computer Science Department for very long because I did not have a PhD, but he assured me that it was no longer a strict requirement and that I was considered a valuable asset to the department. So I started working, permanently, for the IBM San Jose Research Computer Science Department.

1984
Desktop Printer

As I was busy installing the SHERPA control units and my VM/370 software for the printer, Jim King was negotiating with the IBM Boulder printer developers. They were designing a small desktop printer, the IBM 3812 Page Printer. In contrast to the IBM 6670 printer, which was small enough to function as a departmental printer, the 3812 was even smaller and could easily fit in a private office and function as an individual printer. This was a big improvement in convenience from the days when we had to walk to the computer center to pick up our printed output.

Early on in the design Jim King worked with a software engineer in Boulder, Jeff Lotspiech, to define the microcode interface for the IBM 3812. Jim recommended all the microcode commands that were implemented on the SHERPA control unit. He argued for the functions that were necessary to print text, images and graphics on the page, and won most of his arguments.

When the IBM 3812 Page Printer specifications were complete, Jim gave me a copy with the assignment to convert my existing VM/370 software that drove the SHERPA control unit to drive the new interface to the IBM 3812 Page

Printer. Meanwhile the programming staff in Boulder was writing a traditional line printer interface to the 3812.

The command structure and commands were different, but all the function of the SHERPA interface was in the 3812 interface. I wanted some quiet, uninterrupted time to work on converting my existing software, so I arranged to spend some time in the library at the IBM Palo Alto Science Center. Since I lived in Palo Alto, it was a convenient place to work instead of driving an hour on the freeway to IBM in south San Jose.

It did not take me many days to rewrite and test my software for the IBM 3812 Page Printer and I was back at work in San Jose. I installed my rewritten software and we replaced all the SHERPA printers in the building with the new IBM 3812 printers. It was a smooth, transparent transition for the users.

The IBM Computer Science manager, Jim King's manager's manager, was committed to getting the IBM Research ideas into IBM products for the customers in a timely manner. IBM Research was not a product division and did not create, market, or maintain products for customers. Instead, ideally, the research division ideas enhanced and influenced future products from the product divisions. The work Jim King did with the Boulder engineers got the SHERPA function designed into an actual product, the IBM 3812 Page Printer, but the Boulder software support team was focused on the traditional printer applications and was not interested in the additional function designed into the 3812: to print text, image, and graphics on the same page.

Dan Mahoney worked in the Computer Science Department with the explicit responsibility of getting the IBM Research ideas into IBM products. Dan, a former IBM Systems Engineer, had worked closely with marketing and had many contacts. He was instrumental in getting my VM/370 software released as an IBM Program Offering, a product. I was the product owner. I wrote the manuals: an installation guide and a user guide. I responded to customer bugs and issued fixes to the program. I was in the unusual position—unusual for IBM Research—of supporting an IBM product. The product was marketed as the 3812 VM Support Program Offering (5798-DTE). Without the work of Dan Mahoney, this program would have only been available within IBM. I received an IBM Technical Achievement Award for my contribution, an award that came with a small, round, lapel pin inscribed with a labyrinth and a small diamond at the center. This design was chosen by IBM to acknowledge technical achievements and the complexity and intricacies of problem solving.

Maintaining the 3812 VM Support Program did not take much of my time. When I did interact with customers to fix a problem I enjoyed the work, which included talking with the customer, analyzing the situation that caused the problem, finding a fix for the problem, and sending out a new update.

By this time, the construction of the new building around the IBM Research building was complete. We moved from our offices and labs in the trailers into the new addition to the Research building. I had a private, outside office with a window.

John Backus had the office next door to me. I rarely saw John. As an IBM Fellow, he worked independently on his own individual research from his home in San Francisco. I was present at a large reception for John when he received an award. He accepted the award but acknowledged that the work of creating Fortran could not have been done without the other people on the team.

Backus was the winner of the Turing Award[70] in 1977. As I review the list of Turning Award winners I find several winners that I knew from IBM, in particular, Ted Codd (1981), John Cocke (1987) and Jim Gray (1998).

1985
Steep Learning Curve

It was 1985. I now looked for a new assignment. The previous year, 1984, Edmund's children—Todd, now sixteen, Sara, now eleven, and Gavin now eight—came to live with us full time. Since I was commuting to San Jose, it meant that I left the house before 7 a.m. to join my carpool and returned about 6 p.m. IBM had offices and projects in Palo Alto on Page Mill Road and California Avenue and I wanted to work for one of these departments and avoid the long commute and devote more time to my new family.

Jim King was my manager at the time. He arranged for me to work, on loan, for a software project in Palo Alto that was releasing the AIX[71] operating system (based on Unix BSD 4.2[72]) for the soon to be announced IBM RT[73], a desktop computer. My job was to implement the support for the 3812 Page Printer in this environment.

This was a very challenging period of time. In addition to becoming a full-time parent, everything about my assignment was new to me: Unix operating system, C programming language, automatic build systems using makefiles[74], different text processing tools, different font formats and font width tables. Everything was different except the IBM 3812 Page

Printer. I felt like I had moved to a foreign country and was trying to communicate in a language I barely understood. Tasks I could do easily now had to be figured out from the beginning. For example, I knew there must be a way to display the current time, but I did not know what command to use to get the answer.

In addition to the steep learning curve for completing my assignment, I was working with a group of people who were under a tight deadline to get their product developed and announced. I had come from an environment where people took the time to answer your questions. Now I was working with people who were under extreme pressure and resented any interruption. During one of the meetings I looked around the room and noticed the wide range of men and women working on this project. They came from the US, Canada, India, and the Middle East representing different cultural backgrounds and religions, yet they were united and working together to solve the technical problems to create this new IBM product.

Slowly, making many mistakes along the way, I learned this new environment. Once, when I checked-in all my modified routines, I was surprised to discover that none of my functions were included when the system was re-built. The automatic build routines did not find my changes because I had checked my code into the wrong directory tree. I was not steeped in the common knowledge of how the Unix "build" system worked.

On top of this, the computers were overloaded and response time was miserable. The process of checking in my code could take hours. I resorted to returning to work at 10 p.m. (after going home to fix dinner, enjoy a family meal, help the kids with their homework, and participate in bed-time rituals) to get the response time I needed, often staying until 2 a.m. I had thought working closer to home would make everything easier. I would never have returned to work to do a late-night shift if I had a one-hour commute, so in a way, working closer to home had made things more difficult.

As the day neared for the announcement of the new IBM RT workstation, I was shocked by how unprepared we were. My software was still crashing and I did not think the rest of the operating system was in better shape. But the announce-ment was made and everything was treated as a celebration. We had a few months before we had to deliver the product. My colleagues reassured me they had been through this sev-eral times and everything would be in pretty good shape by the ship date. This was "normal" for product divisions, but I found it very stressful.

My stumbling and bumbling along finally yielded re-sults. I navigated the Unix operating system. I modified the Unix printer interface. I accessed the Unix fonts and inter-preted the Unix printer files. I implemented the commands to send Unix documents with Unix fonts to the IBM 3812 Page Printer. It was working. The system was shipped but I had had enough!

I was very glad that Jim King only loaned me to the department in Palo Alto. The pressure of working in that product environment was quite exhausting. I preferred the long commute and a calmer working environment. In spring 1986 I was very happy to return to IBM Research. During my absence, the Research lab had moved to a new location, the IBM Almaden Research Center[75]. This beautiful building is located in the hills between the IBM Cottle Road location and the Almaden Valley.

I had an office of my own with built-in desk and file cabinets and a wall of windows overlooking the entrance plaza. The display terminal and computer in my office connected to a state-of-the-art experimental operating system developed by members in the Computer Science Department. This operating system managed multiple computers and created a distributed computing environment. If I was modifying a programming system and required multiple programs recompiled, it would run the compiles on any computer in anyone's office where cycles were available, thereby completing the tasks in record time.

1986
IBM and Adobe

In 1986, after Adobe Systems had announced PostScript, IBM was about to ask Adobe Systems to write a program to convert files from the IBM text format (AFPDS) to PostScript. Instead, Jim King gave me this assignment, and I wrote the conversion program that translated files from AFPDS to Post-Script. This conversion program allowed the most common IBM text files to be printed on the newly announced Post-Script printers. These printers were part of the desktop publishing revolution that put printers in everyone's office.

This project presented me with several challenging puzzles to solve. Before I began, I attended a daylong class at Adobe Systems focusing on how to write efficient PostScript code. Armed with this new information I set to work.

The biggest challenge of this project was to take a print file formatted with IBM fonts and print it on a printer with Adobe fonts. Adobe fonts were scalable while IBM fonts were designed individually for each different size. To address this, I created two user-modifiable tables. One mapped the IBM font names to the Adobe font names: for each IBM font, it specified the corresponding Adobe font. If the user did not like the mapping I specified, they could modify the table. The second table mapped the IBM font character names, sometimes called glyphs[76], to the corresponding Adobe character names. Again, users could modify this mapping for their own purposes. Using these tables, my conversion program could select the appropriate Adobe font and character for printing.

That solved the problem of mapping from IBM fonts to Adobe fonts, but now I had to contend with the different character widths in the two sets of fonts.

Most text processing applications use the font character widths to determine how to justify the right margin in lines of text. The AFPDS files were formatted using the character widths of the characters in the IBM fonts. I wanted a line of text to take up the same amount of space on the PostScript printer as it did on the IBM printer, so I needed to make some adjustments. I had access to the IBM font character widths but not the Adobe font character widths. Fortunately Post-Script is a programming language, not just a file format, so I could insert routines in the PostScript files to do certain calculations at the time of printing.

My conversion program calculated the width of the line of text, in pixels, using the IBM fonts and saved this value as a variable in the PostScript file. When the file was printed on the PostScript printer, my included routine calculated the width of the line of text using the Adobe fonts and compared that width with the saved variable. This routine then determined the difference in the two widths and inserted more (or less) inter-character space between the characters to make the line come out even. In this way I was able to maintain the right margin justification on the text pages.

I finished the program and named it PREPPS as shorthand for "Prepare PostScript." I made it available within the

IBM Research community. PREPPS was a very useful and popular tool for printing IBM documents on PostScript printers and soon it was used by all the IBM internal locations. I never made it into a program offering so it was not available to IBM customers. I do not know if anyone else did.

I still maintained the 3812 VM Support Program and was notified whenever an IBM customer encountered an error in the program. The computer science management had changed over the last few years and the new management found it strange that I, as a member of the Research Division, was providing technical support for a product. It did not take up much of my time, but now I wanted to put out a new release with a new function. As I recall, the new function involved another way the 3812 Page Printer could be attached to the computer. I could see that the customers wanted this new function, but I could not convince my management to allow me to make the changes and ship an update. This went on for over a year during which time I had several new immediate managers. With each new manager I requested permission to make this modification and ship it to the customers as a product upgrade. Each time the manager continued to reflect the position of the upper management and I was told not to do it. "Research does not support products," they said.

I did not give up on the idea but I did set it aside. I was not the type of employee to directly go against management, and I certainly would not distribute new function to the customer without management approval. At the same time I listened each year when the IBM CEO, John F. Akers, gave his talk to IBM employees over the intercom system. He said that our first responsibility was to respond to the customer requirements. I had heard this message, clearly, over the years from four previous IBM CEOs: Thomas Watson, Jr., T. Vincent Learson, Frank T. Cary, and John R. Opel. Since I knew that the IBM customers wanted this new feature, I felt that I had some support from the top of IBM even if it was not reflected in my immediate management.

When Steve Zilles became my manager I told him that I wanted to release a new version of the 3812 VM Support Program. He immediately approved the project. Now that I had permission it took only about a week to do the technical work to prepare the new version, complete with modified documentation. It was the decision-making process that delayed the release, not the technical complexity of the problem. The new release was readily accepted. After perhaps another year of minor work on the project, the product division in Boulder, Colorado, was finally convinced to pick up the responsibility for maintaining this program offering.

1987-1991
PostScript/Hourglass Software

Jeff Lotspiech, the IBM Boulder engineer who designed the IBM 3812 microcode with Jim King, was now working for Jim King at IBM Research at the Almaden site. They defined an object-oriented[77] graphics interface for display and printer devices. This interface defined functional objects for lines, arcs, fonts, area fill, etc. It was called the Hourglass Language and Image Processing Software for printers and displays. They wanted to know if this graphics interface was robust enough to implement the PostScript language. Jim King gave me the assignment to write a PostScript Interpreter to interface with the Hourglass software. This program was to read a PostScript file, interpret all the PostScript operators, and issue calls to the Hourglass software to create the image of the document on either the display or printer.

If you pick up the two-inch thick PostScript Language Reference manual you will see the definition of the PostScript language with all the various operators: hundreds of operators. How do you eat an elephant? One byte at a time. I started. Soon I had the fundamental operators implemented. All the graphic PostScript operators (fonts, lines, arcs, images) were implemented as calls to the underlying Hourglass software.

One day Jim King walked into my office. "I am leaving IBM to take a position with Adobe Systems," he announced.

I was shocked. How could he leave IBM and the Hourglass project? I had worked with him since the days of the SHERPA project. He had given me so many interesting and challenging projects to work on. It truly was a privilege to be assigned good work where I was able to use my programming talents. What would it have been like to have the skills but no opportunity to apply them? I felt honored to work with him and the shock of his leaving left me speechless. It took me awhile to adjust.

I still had interesting work and excellent colleagues at IBM Research. I continued to implement the PostScript/Hourglass Interpreter and my September 1989 status report indicated my progress: 214 operators written out of the 274 total PostScript operators; 75% complete; 9000 lines of code. Jeff Lotspiech was now the lead on the Hourglass project. The depth of his knowledge was invaluable. Sig Nin also worked on the project. Carol Thompson contributed innovative filters to the file system structure. Steve Zilles, the overall manager, contacted the IBM printer and display divisions in order to transfer the Hourglass technology into IBM products. During this time the Hourglass project members received Research Division Technical Awards for innovation and I was promoted to Senior Programmer, the highest level programming position in IBM.

I implemented all of the PostScript level 1 operators. It is not necessary to describe any of the details of that project. I had fun writing the code and watching more and more of it running. Since the Hourglass software drove either a printer or a display, I tested the majority of my software by displaying the results on a display terminal in my office. I no longer had to debug my code by waiting to see what showed up on the printed page.

One part of the PostScript Interpreter I particularly enjoyed writing was the garbage collection routines. As a PostScript file is processed it allocates variables into a data space. But it does not explicitly free the data space when the data is no longer needed. The logic for this routine challenged me as I designed a method to determine what data was still "alive" and built a table. Then my routine compressed the data to remove the "garbage" data and rewrote the data back into the memory, updating all the data references to reflect the new locations. This was a complex routine but satisfying to figure out.

When I worked on a long, complex problem and it was time to catch my carpool to go home, I would leave a short note telling myself what to do next. Then my mind was free to focus on home and family. When I returned the next day I could quickly pick up where I left off and by the time I'd finished that next step my mind was re-engaged with the whole problem. In this way I jump-started my problem-solving thinking.

I continued to commute from Palo Alto to south San Jose with my carpool. We were an eleven-person carpool that met before 7 a.m. at the Mitchel Park Library. When we gathered we would look around and decide how many cars to take since sometimes there would be only six or eight of us carpooling that day. We kept track of how many rides and how many drives each person accumulated to keep things even.

One day while driving the carpool to work, I started to feel very uncomfortable, as if I was going to faint. I pulled off the freeway and had someone else finish the drive. This was a very strange experience that left me shaken. Another time, in the hallway at work, I felt a sudden loss of energy followed by extreme fatigue. For months, while I investigated these symptoms, I did not drive on the freeway and fortunately, because of the carpool, I was able to get to and from IBM and keep working. Eventually I was able to resume driving and catch up on my drives for the carpool.

Around this time Jim King, now working at Adobe Systems, began a discussion with me about going to work at Adobe. "These people think like you do," he concluded. "You would like working in this environment."

Yes, I thought, but at the same time I was facing these unknown symptoms. Just when I thought I was feeling better and could apply myself to a new challenge, the symptoms of fatigue hit me again, knocking me off my feet. My doctors could find nothing wrong, which was reassuring, but something felt "off" in my system. I consulted an Ayurveda doctor who recognized that my body was out of balance and prescribed a diet more fitting to my constitution. Slowly, over time, I got better but I never followed up on the possibility of working for Adobe.

In 1991 Adobe announced PostScript Level 2 and I started implementing the new operators. Then, with the PostScript/Hourglass software written and debugged, we approached the IBM printer and display divisions to use our software in their devices. We met only moderate success. Some of the Hourglass ideas were accepted by the product divisions, but they were reluctant to pick up the PostScript interpreter. The product division managers were more inclined to license the Adobe System PostScript software for the printers. This involved large royalties to Adobe Systems.

Things were changing at IBM in other ways. More work was contracted to external organizations as opposed to being done in-house. I watched this trend with apprehension. Then IBM started to downsize. Offers for early retirement were made every year. Every year I considered it.

1991
My IBM 25th Anniversary

In June of 1991 I reached my twenty-fifth anniversary with IBM. This was always a celebrated milestone. Each IBM employee who reached twenty-five years was given a budget for a celebration and a gift to be selected from a catalog. The budget was enough for four to six people to have a celebratory dinner at an up-scale restaurant. I had attended several of these dinners for other IBMers; now it was time for me to plan my own celebration. When I thought back over my career and the people who had been important to me, there were many more than four that I wanted to invite. I decided to have a luncheon instead.

The IBM Almaden Research cafeteria had a BBQ lunch once a week and the price was such that I could invite twenty-five people. This was a very special luncheon for me and I invited people from many of my former IBM projects along with my current colleagues. Also I invited my Aunt Lois and Uncle Lee, without whose support I would never have had the opportunity to attend the University of Washington and earn my degree in mathematics. My brother John was at the UW during the same years when I lived with my aunt and uncle. He and his wife Rose Marie attended. Edmund was there. My former roommate, from when I first arrived at

IBM, Cathy Jones Priest, was there. The librarians from the LMS project were there.

The luncheon was held in the IBM cafeteria conference room. As we sat around the long table, I realized that I knew everyone from the different phases of my career but that they did not all know one another and their importance to me. When the meal was over I was presented with the gift I had selected: a set of silver-plated flatware. Then I took the floor. I walked around the room and stopped behind each person's chair. I introduced each person and said when we had worked together and something about the project. I am so glad that I did this because it seemed to unite the room and everyone could see how my career wove together with everyone present. I was very appreciative to everyone I had worked with.

I received a notebook of letters from colleagues acknowledging this milestone. It is a wonderful collection of letters with lots of memories. Here is an excerpt from a letter written by a colleague when I was on loan to the Unix project in Palo Alto. I appreciate his kind and perceptive words:

I would like to add my voice to the throng of congratulations on your 25th anniversary at IBM. I look back and have fond memories of shared experiences. I recall code reviews of some strange daemon, a denizen of the deep, a 3812 printer daemon.

Mostly I think of you and remember honesty and enthusiasm. I wish to thank you for your support and help, for your integrity and consistency to a vision of what an individual can accomplish within an organization that often seems fraught with peril.

You are a special person. I believe that you are in touch with the spirit of goodness. I have seen your inner strength shine and hope that some day I may contribute to that world which you see, a beautiful understanding and caring world.

Congratulations!

Here is excerpt from another letter written by Jeff Lotspiech. Jeff formatted his letter of congratulations in the IBM time honored tradition of releasing "Frequently Asked Questions" with any announcement.

Q: Occasionally we hear people who knew Katherine in the old days refer to her as "Kathy Hitchcock." What is the story here?

A: This is a complete mystery. Records show that long ago there was a Kathy Hitchcock at the Los Gatos Laboratory, but the current best theory is that she was an entirely different person.

Q: How come Katherine always leaves work at 4:00 pm?

A: Katherine belongs to a carpool that arrives early and thus leaves early. However, this is largely a matter of conjecture, since no on else arrives early enough to verify this.

I treasure these letters from my colleagues on my twenty-fifth anniversary.

Another year went by; I was working on PostScript Level 2 operators when IBM made another early retirement offer. The offer was too good to refuse. Still I debated it, wondering what it would be like to leave IBM. The offer provided full retirement benefits for anyone who had thirty years with the company. I did not qualify for that. But another part of the offer provided a five-year bridge to retirement. If you left IBM after twenty-five years you would continue to accrue your years until you reached thirty years when you could draw your full retirement. This was truly a golden handshake. I would need to work somewhere during those five years, but afterwards I would have my full IBM retirement. I discussed the decision with Edmund. He left it up to me.

With IBM hiring so many contract programmers, I felt that I could easily get a contracting position with IBM. Finally I made my decision to take the bridge to retirement. When I announced it to my colleagues I discovered that several others were taking advantage of the same opportunity. In particular Carol Thompson, from the Hourglass project, and Irene Beardsley, my carpool buddy, announced their plans to retire the same day I did.

I immediately hired on with a contracting firm that supplied IBM with programmers. I did not miss a day of work because I was assigned back on the same project: the PostScript/Hourglass software. Carol also rejoined the project as a contract programmer.

Things were changing at home also. Edmund's children were growing up and going their separate ways. Todd had recently married his high school sweetheart, Samantha. The kids' mother and stepfather moved to Bellingham, Washington and when Sara graduated from high school she moved with them. Gavin was the only one still at home. He stayed one year more, and then chose to move to Bellingham at the beginning of his junior year of high school. Soon we had an empty nest. Edmund was busy dreaming and searching for the perfect boat.

1992-2001
Contract Programmer

As a contract programmer to IBM I continued to work on the PostScript Interpreter interface to the Hourglass software.

Early in 1993, Edmund and I found and purchased the perfect boat, *Volant*, a 38' steel-hulled sailboat, in St. Petersburg, Florida. In December of 1993 I let my contract lapse and we took a six-month cruise from St. Petersburg to Key West to Miami to the Bahamas and back to Florida. We returned to California in July 1994 with plans for another trip the following winter. I did not go back to contracting work when we returned, but as the year progressed it became apparent that our next trip would be delayed and our finances depended on my working also. I hired back as a contract programmer with Almaden Research with a specific assignment to test the PostScript level 2 Interpreter.

The testing process involved a test suite of PostScript Level 2 programs. Because the Hourglass software interfaced to the display units, I could do all the testing without a printer. As I began work on this project, Edmund and I realized that we could not leave our boat unattended in Florida while we lived and worked in California, so Edmund arranged to continue his contract programming work from the boat in Florida. I arranged with my manager, Robin Williams, to continue my program testing work remotely. Since Robin wanted me to work at an IBM facility, he contacted an IBM PC manager in Boca Raton and arranged for me to be temporarily located in their offices. The Boca Raton management provided me with an office, a computer, a display, a printer, and colleagues. My reputation proceeded me as my Boca Raton colleagues knew and used programs I had written, in particular the software for the IBM 3812 printer and PREPPS: the software to convert IBM print files to PostScript files.

Edmund and I moved the boat, our jobs, and ourselves to Ft. Lauderdale in the spring of 1995. I commuted about an hour from Ft. Lauderdale to Boca Raton and continued the systematic testing of the Level 2 PostScript operators. A couple of times I traveled to IBM in Rochester, Minnesota to provide training on the PostScript/Hourglass software as they worked to include it in their product plans.

The large IBM Boca Raton site was in the process of downsizing. A year later it closed and all the work was transferred to Austin, Texas. My colleagues were either transferring or finding other jobs. I needed to find another IBM location where I could work. I found an IBM group that was located in an office building near Cypress Creek Road that was less than half the commute to Boca Raton.

June 1996 was my thirtieth anniversary working at IBM. I was now officially retired from IBM, but I continued to work through a contracting agency as a programmer for IBM Almaden Research. We were saving our funds for an extended cruise in 1998.

I completed the testing of the Level 2 Interpreter in 1997 and stopped working on the project. Edmund and I took a year and half cruise on our sailboat, *Volant,* through the Caribbean, returning to Florida in June of 1999.

In the fall, after we returned, I talked with Jeff Lotspiech from Almaden Research and learned about an IBM project in Ft. Lauderdale that was using some of the software from the Hourglass project, in particular the file filter system. Jeff consulted with this group on a regular basis. He arranged an interview for me and soon I started to work directly for that group as a contract programmer. This time I was able to work through Edmund's contract programming business, Downing Associated Incorporated (DAI).

This IBM project in Ft. Lauderdale was developing software to download music to individuals' personal computers. It was a project in association with music companies. The focus was on distributing music but only to the computers where the music was purchased. There were safeguards to prevent pirating music.

I knew the Hourglass file filter system used to encode, compress, and write the music data across the Internet to the user's computer. My first responsibility was to add a new filter into the output stream. I had been away from programming for two years while we were sailing. Now the first thing I did was open up a program to modify it. In the program code I found notes that I had written three years earlier when I was debugging one of the filters. I was back in a familiar environment.

We were creating software routines to distribute music files anywhere in the world via the Internet. These files contained highly encoded and compressed data. These files could have contained anything. I was asked to insert a filter that would write a decoding key into the music files to allow them to be decompressed and inspected in case there were legal or national security questions that required knowing the exact contents of the file.

My filter wrote header information into the file prior to transmitting it across the network. If the network went down or the transmission was terminated for some reason, the filter system would retransmit the data from the point where it had failed. My filter routines needed to calculate the restart position to account for the extra header data. If I made a mistake in this calculation, then the music could have a hiccup where the retransmission occurred. I imagined all the possible scenarios as I developed my routines.

My project leader on this project had previously worked on an assignment at IBM Almaden Research in California. Now he was one of the most knowledgeable project leaders on this music project. He and his wife were fond of California and wanted to return. He took note of the time when I had lived in Florida, where I wanted to live, and worked remotely for Almaden, in California. He wanted to do the reverse. He wanted to continue the work he was doing for the music project in Florida but he wanted to live in Palo Alto, California. Encouraged by what I had done, he soon made the arrangements and announced that he and his wife were moving to California. He would have his office at Almaden Research and he would continue working on the music project in Ft Lauderdale. Of course, as time went by, he found a new IBM project in California.

I continued to work for this project until March of 2001, when Edmund and I took a six-month cruise on *Volant* from Ft. Lauderdale to Nova Scotia and back. We returned in December 2001. I was still employed by the project when I returned from this trip. This was quite a compliment to me since most of the other contract employees had been let go.

In January 2002, after a few weeks internal debate, I decided not to go back to work. The decision was difficult because I always enjoyed the challenge of writing computer programs. But on the other hand, I could see that the changing technology was getting ahead of me. Plus, the demands, challenges and opportunities of sailing were taking more and more of my time and interest. As I looked at Edmund's and my plans for 2002, which included boat repair and sailing with friends in Sweden, I noticed that I did not have a contiguous block of time to commit to working. Finally, I called and talked to my IBM manager to express my appreciation that they had kept a position open for me and told them that I was not going to take it. Thus ended my thirty-five years of working at IBM.

Epilogue

When Edmund and I bought our boat and started cruising, we decided that our full names were much too formal for this cruising lifestyle. Also, we had just read the account of a sailor who fell overboard when his wife was below and off watch. He yelled out his wife's name: "Pam!" as he fell. Suddenly our names seemed too complicated for such an emergency situation. We chose nicknames. Edmund chose Bear, from when he was called "little bear" as a child. I choose Kit, another of the many variations on Katherine. I no longer felt like Kathy and I did not feel like a Kate, Katie or Kat. So we were Kit and Bear of *Volant*. Among cruisers you rarely know people's last name, usually only their boat name.

I have stayed in touch with a few of my ASDD colleagues from the time we worked together in 1968 and 1969 on the Library Management System (LMS). I saw Alice McMullen in 2001 when Bear and I sailed up the East Coast. She visited us for an evening on our boat in a harbor near Cape Fear, North Carolina. I learned that when Alice retired from IBM she never used computers again, even though personal computers were popular.

In June of 2003 we sailed *Volant* for a month in the Bahamas then shipped her to Vancouver, B.C., via Dock Wise. That August we docked *Volant* in front of the Empress Hotel in Victoria, and invited Marjorie Griffin (the inspiration for the library project) to join us for lunch. Marjorie was walking with a walker at the time but managed to climb the few steps up to the cockpit to share an afternoon aboard with us. On a later visit with her at her retirement facility we phoned and talked with Vi Ma and Caryl McAllister also from the days of the library project in 1969. Alice and Marjorie have now passed away. I continue to share Christmas greetings with Vi Ma.

In 2005, Bear passed away after fighting cancer for over two years. It was sudden and shocking even though I knew he was not going to win against this disease. He was optimistic and frequently said that "the only difference between ordeal and adventure is attitude." He was on the water, teaching sailing, up to his last days.

2006
Afterword:
Forty-Year Retrospective

In 2006 I was in San Jose and arranged to meet some of my former IBM colleagues for lunch at the IBM Almaden Research Center. Since I was visiting a friend in south San Jose I did not use my normal approach on the US 101 freeway but turned south onto Monterey Highway near the IBM Cottle Road facility. Seeing the stately trees that divide the highway, trees that were planted during the time of the California missions, I had a flood of memories from when I first drove down the highway forty years earlier to interview for a job at IBM. Reflecting on that day, in my senior year at the university and my subsequent decision to accept the IBM job offer, I pondered how everything had turned out.

As I continued down Monterey Highway, and turned right at the entrance to IBM on Cottle Road, I was startled to see a Hitachi sign next to the IBM sign. I noted this as I continued on my way a few more miles before I turned up into the foothills and approached the Almaden Lab. At the entrance there were also two signs: IBM and Hitachi. What did this mean? I had been away from IBM for a number of years and I was not following IBM news.

I walked into the lobby of the IBM Almaden Research Lab and saw a large, celebratory display acknowledging the 50th anniversary of the Random Access Disk Technology developed by IBM engineers in San Jose. "50 years," I mused to myself, "and I was here forty years ago, very close to the beginning." The invention of the disk technology had led to the construction of the IBM Cottle Road facility.

I left the lobby and walked down the wide hallway toward the cafeteria, floor to ceiling glass windows on my right and beautiful blue/green tile under my feet. On the wall to the left were a row of plaques with photos and descriptions of people who had recently received IBM Outstanding Technical Achievement Awards or Research Division Awards. I smiled, remembering when I had been the recipient.

In the cafeteria I joined my colleagues, several of whom I had known and worked with for over twenty-five years. At lunch, I asked about the Hitachi signs and I learned that IBM had sold its magnetic disk drive business to Hitachi. What a surprise! This sale took place in January 2003. I was deeply involved at that time caring for my husband and was not paying attention to the news. This was the first I knew that IBM had sold the disk technology.

Fifty years after its invention—fifty years of continuing innovations and improvements[78]—IBM no longer owns the magnetic disk drive technology. I thought about how close I was to its beginning since I started at IBM just ten years after its invention and knew the manager and some of the engineers who invented this technology.

After the luncheon I returned to my car and again drove along Monterey Highway. Time has brought forty years of changes to me and to IBM. Only the trees growing in the center divide of the Monterey Highway seemed unchanged.

Computer technology continues to change at a rapid pace. When I first decided to become a computer programmer, when I first saw remote computing, I wanted computers to provide the answers at our fingertips. I never envisioned the wireless network of handheld devices that we have today.

In retrospect, I used very little of the mathematics classes that I studied at the University of Washington. Mostly I used my logic and problem solving skills. I liked writing and debugging programs. It fit well with my logical thinking patterns. Each program was like a challenging puzzle to be solved as I thought ahead to all the possible situations and wrote routines to handle each one of them. When there was a bug or crash, I constructed a test case to isolate the problem down to the faulty logic or condition that had not been foreseen. There was always the satisfaction when something was first up and running or when a bug was fixed. It met my need for results.

Early in my IBM career when the library project was cancelled and I was struggling with the challenges of the meaning of life, at the brink of a discouraging attitude, another employee said to me, "You will get used to the disappointments and give up on your ideals." I wondered when and if this would happen to me. Fortunately there were several turning points in my career and lessons learned that carried me onward into exciting and challenging projects. I not only found my way but also actively participated in creating my way during this time of rapidly changing technology.

Some people, when they look back on their career, remember maybe one outstanding project in terms of rewarding work and excellent colleagues. It is with satisfaction that I look back and see a half dozen or more of such projects where I worked alongside extraordinary people.

In Appreciation

I wish to thank Reingard Rieger for her enthusiastic suggestion that I write my IBM stories. As I began, Joanne Horn provided valuable guidance when I attended her class: *Second Half Connections*. Thanks to Nancy Wick, from *Enlightened Edits*, for her review and useful comments on my first version.

I greatly appreciate Karen Kettlety who made a time and place for me to write on her lovely sheep ranch in eastern Oregon.

Early readers of my stories have offered encouragement and thoughtful suggestions. These include Les Hitchcock, Susanna Rojas, Jeff Hitchcock, Linda Allen, and Andy Seligman. Thank you all.

I appreciate Toni Burmeister and Pat Charlson for our informal writing group and for their listening. Thanks to Sandy Farrell for periodically asking: "How is the writing going?" and to Carol Pearl for her continued interest.

Special thanks to my stepchildren: Todd Downing who, with all his writing, producing and publishing, has been an inspiration; Sara Nolan who shares my deep interest in reading; and Gavin Downing who, along with his wife Michelle, felt that I had an important story to tell.

I am forever grateful to my women's group in Eugene, Oregon, and the path we have traveled together: Deborah

Aikens, Renée Taylor, Susanne deSandre, Linda Sattler, Linda Weaver, and especially Dana Davis who listened, daily, as I made my writing goals.

I wish to recognize Eva Long, with Long on Books, for her valuable editing and guidance on this path to publishing.

Thanks to Jacqueline Thurston for her perceptive friendship through all my career years, beginning in 1968, and beyond.

Finally, with great appreciation, I thank my IBM colleagues.

My parents and siblings in June 1966 when John and I graduated from the University of Washington. Left to right: Les, John, my dad, Luther, Keith, my mother, Melinda and me.

John and me with Aunt Lois and Uncle Lee on the day of our graduation from the University of Washington.

Fellow IBM programmer and roommate, Cathy Jones, and me on a ski trip to Lake Tahoe, 1967.

Three photographs of me at the IBM Advanced Systems Development Division (ASDD) 1968, 1969, and 1970.

The redwood and glass building where I worked in the Advanced Systems Development Division (ASDD) of IBM.

The Hitchcock Formula: 1 Ton IBM Paper = 17 Trees

KATHERINE Hitchcock's intense interest in conservation grows out of a life crowded with outdoor activities. The 26-year-old programmer at the Advanced Systems Development Division laboratory in Los Gatos takes frequent back-packing trips into the majestic solitude of the High Sierras, and on a recent vacation she spent two weeks hiking across the French and Swiss Alps.

Last year, she found a way to return something to nature: When she saw some of the piles of records IBM has had to store as a result of the antitrust suits, she started thinking about the tons of paper IBM uses every day. "It occurred to me," she says, "that IBM could start a conservation trend in the data processing world by finding a way to re-cycle printout paper."

Inspired by the fact that 20 percent of all paper produced in the United States is derived from recycled waste paper, Miss Hitchcock —a member of the Sierra Club and Ecology Action, two California conservation groups—searched Northern California for a processing company interested in buying IBM's cut-dated, non-confidential printout paper. The search ended in success.

"Printout is just the kind of waste the commercial processors are looking for," says Miss Hitchcock. "It's very compact, already separated from other kinds of waste, and easy to process in a pulping operation."

Once she had all the facts, she submitted her re-cycling plan through the IBM Suggestion Program, and it was adopted. The result: Her idea has been implemented not only by the Los Gatos ASDD lab, but also by the Systems Manufacturing Division plant and Research and Systems Development Division laboratories at San Jose, as well as the SMD plant and SDD laboratory at Boulder, and at the Poughkeepsie lab. At Poughkeepsie, which started its re-cycling program early in March, an eight-week's collection produced 80 to 100 tons of paper for re-cycling. SMD Poughkeepsie has just initiated a similar program.

Today, these locations produce about 65 tons of waste printout for re-cycling every month. In addition, data processing centers at Stanford University and the University of California at Berkeley have launched similar programs.

The woman who started it all reports with delight: "For every ton of paper that's re-cycled, seventeen trees are saved from cutting." ■

Think 43

Article in the IBM *Think* magazine, June 1971, about my recycling program.

Los Gatos programmer Kathy Hitchcock had the solution in hand when the energy crisis struck in earnest this winter. For several years she had argued that car pools made sense, economically, ecologically, and even socially. Her program, written for the Model 65, came out of mothballs and formed the basis of carpooling efforts in Los Gatos-San Jose.

Article in *IBM NEWS*, February 25, 1974, about my carpool program.

My IBM badges and ID cards over the years:

Clockwise starting on top right: Systems Development Division (SDD) from 1973; General Products Division (GPD) 1976; SDD 1974; IBM ID card 1976; IBM ID card 1970; IBM ID card 1984; SDD 1974; SDD 1975; IBM ID card 1972. Center: Research Division 1977.

Edmund Downing and me aboard the Redwood Coast, 1980.

Todd, Gavin and Sara when I first met them in 1980.

Sara, Todd and Gavin on one of our ski holidays.

Family portrait of Edmund, Sara, Todd, Gavin and me in 1987.

Jim King, Ben Milander, me, Sig Nin and George Swanson all standing behind the IBM 6670 with the SHERPA Control Unit sitting on the top right side.

Jim King and me with IBM 3812 Page Printer.

Dan Mahoney, Brad Wade, Debra Fenzel-Alexandra and Jeff Lotspiech
at my twenty-fifth anniversary luncheon on June 27, 1991.

Almaden Research Center colleagues at my twenty-fifth anniversary
luncheon. Left-to-right: Robin Williams, Michael Cooper, Steve Zilles,
Jim McCrossin, Carol Thompson, Jeff Lotspiech, me, Ben Milander and
Sajhi Birk.

Hourglass Project members photographed when we were honored with awards. I received a Research Division Technical Award for my contribution. Standing left to right: Jim McCrossin, Robin Williams, Duaine Pryor, Jeff Lotspiech and Steve Zilles. Seated: Sig Nin, Carol Thompson and me.

Marjorie
Griffin

'Bear' and 'Kit' with Marjorie Griffin (far right) and her sailing buddy Judy, Victoria, B.C. in September 2003. Insert: Photo of Marjorie from 1968 when she was the inspiration for the library automation project.

Volant anchored in the Bahamas, June 2003.

Notes and Links

These Internet links are provided as a convenience to the reader who may wish more information about the technology and/or the individuals reference in this book. As with the nature of the Internet, there is no guarantee that, over time, the links will remain valid.

Disclaimer: The publisher is not responsible for websites (or their content) that are not owned by the publisher.

1. Link to BASIC: http://en.wikipedia.org/wiki/BASIC

2. Link to fan-fold: http://en.wikipedia.org/wiki/Fan-fold

3. Link to Dr. Sharpe's autobiography at the Nobel Prize website: http://www.nobelprize.org/nobel_prizes/economics/laureates/1990/sharpe-autobio.html

4. Link to RAMAC: http://en.wikipedia.org/wiki/IBM_305_RAMAC

5. Link to IBM 1401: http://en.wikipedia.org/wiki/IBM_1401

6. Link to batch jobs: http://en.wikipedia.org/wiki/Batch_processing

7. Link to Autocoder: http://en.wikipedia.org/wiki/Autocoder

8. Link to bill of materials: http://en.wikipedia.org/wiki/Bill_of_materials

9. Link to flowchart: http://en.wikipedia.org/wiki/Flow_chart

10. Link to IBM System 360 Operating System: http://en.wikipedia.org/wiki/OS/360

11. Link to IBM 2260 display terminal: http://en.wikipedia.org/wiki/IBM_2260

12. Link to Rey Johnson: http://en.wikipedia.org/wiki/Rey_Johnson

13. This same concern for the cost of data storage led many computer application designers to store only the last two digits of the year (storing 1968 as 68) which led to the Y2K computer concerns.

14. Link to search engines: http://en.wikipedia.org/wiki/Search_engine_(computing)

15. Link to Google: http://en.wikipedia.org/wiki/Google_Search

16. Link to Sempervirens Fund: http://sempervirens.org/

17. I recently contacted the Sempervirens Fund to see if they could confirm the amount of this donation but they could not.

18. Link to Operations Research: http://en.wikipedia.org/wiki/Operations_research

19. Link to Doug Engelbart: http://en.wikipedia.org/wiki/Douglas_Engelbart

20. Link to computer mouse: http://en.wikipedia.org/wiki/Mouse_(computing)

21. Link to article about Ernie Nassimbene: http://langsquare.exblog.jp/8257663/

22. Link to microcode: http://en.wikipedia.org/wiki/Microcode

23. Link to IBM 3614: http://en.wikipedia.org/wiki/IBM_3624

24. Link to rotary dial: http://en.wikipedia.org/wiki/Rotary_dial

25. Link to floppy disk: http://en.wikipedia.org/wiki/Floppy_disk

26. Link to booting: http://en.wikipedia.org/wiki/Bootstrapping

27. Link to flash drives: http://en.wikipedia.org/wiki/Flash_drives

28. Link to Queuing Theory: http://en.wikipedia.org/wiki/Queueing_theory

29. Link to HP-35 calculator: http://en.wikipedia.org/wiki/HP-35

30. Link to Why Man Creates: http://en.wikipedia.org/wiki/Why_Man_Creates

31. I just looked up this film and found it described on Wikipedia. My quotes are very close to the actual lines in the film that are documented in the section called digression. But I leave mine unchanged, reflecting my memory.

32. The Personnel Department with its responsibilities is now called Human Resources.

33. Link to 1973 oil embargo: http://en.wikipedia.org/wiki/Oil_embargo_crisis

34. Link to Jacqueline Grennan Wexler: http://www.hunter.cuny.edu/communications/news/top-featured-stories/hunter-mourns-the-loss-of-former-president-jacqueline-grennan-wexler/?searchterm=Jacqueline

35. Link to IBM Research Division: http://en.wikipedia.org/wiki/IBM_Research

36. Link to IBM Yorktown Heights: http://en.wikipedia.org/wiki/Thomas_J._Watson_Research_Center

37. Link to Ted Codd: http://en.wikipedia.org/wiki/Ted_Codd

38. Link to relational model: http://en.wikipedia.org/wiki/Relational_model

39. Link to SEQUEL: http://en.wikipedia.org/wiki/SEQUEL

40. Link to John Backus: http://en.wikipedia.org/wiki/John_Backus

41. Link to IBM Fellow: http://en.wikipedia.org/wiki/IBM_Fellow

42. Link to Fortran: http://en.wikipedia.org/wiki/Fortran

43. Link to Future Systems: http://en.wikipedia.org/wiki/IBM_Future_Systems_project

44. Quote by Dave Sowa found in: http://en.wikipedia.org/wiki/IBM_Future_Systems_project

45. Link to IBM 3800: http://en.wikipedia.org/wiki/IBM_3800

46. Link to MVS: http://en.wikipedia.org/wiki/
    MVS%23MVS.2F370

47. Link to spooling: http://en.wikipedia.org/wiki/Spooling

48. Link to Job Entry Subsystem: http://en.wikipedia.org/wiki/
    Job_Entry_Subsystem_2/3

49. Link to MVT: http://en.wikipedia.org/wiki/OS/360_and_
    successors#MVT

50. Link to Houston Automatic Spooling Priority: http://
    en.wikipedia.org/wiki/Houston_Automatic_Spooling_
    Priority

51. Link to line printer: http://en.wikipedia.org/wiki/Line_
    printer

52. Link to Iron Mountain: http://www.ironmountain.com

53. Link to Annapurna: http://en.wikipedia.org/wiki/Annapurna

54. Link to Arlene Blum: http://en.wikipedia.org/wiki/Arlene_
    Blum

55. Link to IBM Selectric typewriter: http://en.wikipedia.org/
    wiki/IBM_Selectric_typewriter

56. Link to Versatec: http://en.wikipedia.org/wiki/Electrofax

57. Link to VM/CMS: http://en.wikipedia.org/wiki/VM/CMS

58. Link to CMS EXEC: http://en.wikipedia.org/wiki/CMS_
    EXEC

59. Link to raster graphic image: http://en.wikipedia.org/wiki/
    Raster_graphics

60. Link to bitmap: http://en.wikipedia.org/wiki/Bitmap

61. Link to pixels: http://en.wikipedia.org/wiki/Pixel

62. Link to all-points-addressable: http://en.wikipedia.org/wiki/
    All_Points_Addressable

63. Link to AFPDS: http://publib.boulder.ibm.com/infocenter/ iseries/v5r3/index.jsp?topic=/rzalu/rzaluafpds.htm

64. Link to Adobe Systems: http://en.wikipedia.org/wiki/Adobe_ Systems

65. Link to PostScript: http://en.wikipedia.org/wiki/PostScript

66. Link to Xerox Research Park: http://en.wikipedia.org/wiki/ Xerox_PARC

67. Link to Apple, Inc: http://en.wikipedia.org/wiki/Apple_Inc.

68. Link to Desktop publishing: http://en.wikipedia.org/wiki/ Desktop_publishing

69. Link to CP-40: http://en.wikipedia.org/wiki/CP-40

70. Link to Turing: http://en.wikipedia.org/wiki/Turing_Award

71. Link to AIX: http://en.wikipedia.org/wiki/IBM_AIX

72. Link to Unix BSD 4.2: http://en.wikipedia.org/wiki/ Berkeley_Software_Distribution

73. Link to IBM RT: http://en.wikipedia.org/wiki/IBM_6150_RT

74. Link to a description of Make and makefiles: http:// en.wikipedia.org/wiki/Make_(software)

75. Link to IBM Almaden Research Center: http://en.wikipedia. org/wiki/IBM_Almaden_Research_Center

76. Link to glyphs: http://en.wikipedia.org/wiki/Glyph

77. Link to object-oriented: http://en.wikipedia.org/wiki/Object- oriented_design

78. Link to history of IBM magnetic disk drive technology: http://en.wikipedia.org/wiki/History_of_IBM_magnetic_ disk_drives

Made in the USA
Columbia, SC
06 March 2021

33986590R00102